Emissary of Love

Also by James F. Twyman

Emissary of Light: A Vision of Peace

Portrait of the Master

Emissary of Love

▼

JAMES F. TWYMAN

Foreword by Neale Donald Walsch

WALSCH
W
BOOKS

an imprint of
HAMPTON ROADS
PUBLISHING COMPANY, INC.
www.hrpub.com

Cover design: KSO Design
Cover Photo: Digital Imagery© Copyright 2002 PhotoDisc, Inc.

Hampton Roads Publishing Company, Inc.
1125 Stoney Ridge Road
Charlottesville, VA 22902

434-296-2772
fax: 434-296-5096
e-mail: hrpc@hrpub.com
www.hrpub.com

If you are unable to order this book from your local
bookseller, you may order directly from the publisher.
Call 1-800-766-8009, toll-free.

Library of Congress Catalog Card Number: 2001099310
ISBN 1-57174-323-5
10 9 8 7 6 5 4 3 2 1

Printed on acid-free paper in Canada

DEDICATION

This book is dedicated to my daughter, Angela,
who has taught me some of the most essential lessons of my life.

FOREWORD

Great truth often comes to us in the form of good stories. With all really good stories there is always a lingering question about the experiences related. Did they really happen? Did they occur in exactly the way they are said to have occurred? Has embellishment played a role in the power and attractiveness of the story? Does any of this matter, or is the wisdom that the story imparts what really matters?

Emissary of Love is a really good story. It has wonderful wisdom to impart. I am not surprised, for the person telling the story is a human being of great compassion and deep insight. His presence is always healing. His soul is always singing the song of love.

James Twyman is not your ordinary storyteller. He is a true sage, one who has found a way to make ancient truth sound new again. He has done so in his life through story and song, carrying messages of wonder and light to souls in search of both. As such, he is a bringer of the light, and an emissary of love.

For many years now James has traveled the world, carrying with him his musical instruments, singing songs of serenity in places of conflict. He has acquired a worldwide reputation as The Peace Troubadour, and is now constantly invited ("begged" is often a more accurate word) by the people of war-torn regions to travel to their land and bring his healing energy, to sing at a time of sorrow, to praise and raise the spirit at a time of its falling, to speak great Truth at a time when every false thought about humans and who they are is on display.

I have watched James do this and marveled at his energy and dedication. And I have had numerous occasions to work side by side with James on the same stage in front of an audience, and to witness his extraordinary effect on the mood of the moment. He can shift the energy in any space toward peace of mind and emergence of the soul's softest expression of love faster than anyone I have ever known.

I have a special nickname for Jimmy Twyman, which I use in the privacy of my own mind. I call him Abbara. As in *abbara-cad-abbarah*. Because he is like a magic spell. And his special magic, which is turning sadness into love, is just the trick right now for a world reeling in disbelief and anguish over man's inhumanity to man.

And now comes, from this special person, a special story. It is a story right out of James Twyman's personal experience. Or is it? Has he made it all up? Is it a figment of his imagination? Has he stretched the truth here and there? Or is it his exact experience, down to the last dotted *i*?

Like the age of a fascinating woman, that is a question one never asks a Master Storyteller. In either instance the question is irrelevant, and the wise one knows it.

No, no, the question is not, Could this really have happened? The question is, What can I learn from this? What treasure was this story placed in my hands to bring me?

Oh, yes, this story *was* placed in your hands. Make no mistake about that. You were meant to read it. Know this: every event is an instruction. We are given an opportunity by each moment in Life to remember something. Something about what we've always known, but have forgotten.

And every so often the world sends our way a Blessed Reminderer. This is usually a person who remembers a bit more about this or that than we do, and who has been chosen to remind us, so that we, too, may remember. These people give us back to ourselves.

James Twyman is such a person.

He knows. He remembers. He understands. And he spends a great deal of his life energy placing before willing and hungry souls his gift of remembrance.

So come, then, and dine on this food for the soul. Come, feast at the Table of the Tale. Take in this wonderful, enchanting, mystical story, and nourish your spirit.

You will be enriched, enlarged, and enlivened.

Neale Donald Walsch

CHAPTER ONE

MARCO

Extraordinary events are often hidden within the wings of very ordinary moments, like rare birds that fly into your life without ever being noticed, as if you've forgotten that they don't belong in the city, or in the mountains, or wherever it is you find yourself on that particular day. But then one bird lands softly upon the sill outside your bedroom window, and you notice something that at first doesn't seem possible. A single breath passes through your lips and an instant later all the tumblers fall into place, and you find yourself considering things you never would have before. There is a gift carried upon those remarkable wings, unmentioned at first, but it changes your life forever. An ordinary bird, but a new world suddenly opens before you. Nothing will ever be the same again, and everyone sees it in your eyes.

I was sitting at the kitchen table eating my breakfast just as I do every morning when I happen to be home, which at last estimate is only around forty percent of the time. It was the end of January 2001, and I had just finished a month-long concert and lecture tour straight down the West Coast, from Seattle to California. Twenty-three gigs in twenty-five days, an ordinary month for a rock star but not for an author/musician known by only a handful of New-Age types. I needed a rest, and I was surprised that I was even awake at 9 A.M. The tour had been a grueling marathon of book signings, peace rallies and evening events. I was finally home, and it felt better than I thought it would.

That's when everything in my life changed.

I was eating a bowl of yogurt and granola, staring out the kitchen window at the birds feasting on the seeds someone poured into the St. Francis feeder. A spoon was balanced lightly in my left hand and I wasn't really paying attention to it, at least not then. All I really cared about were the sparrows that hopped around one another with light agility, tapping their beaks sharply upon the generous bowl St. Francis held in his ceramic hands, that and the coffee brewing on a nearby counter. It was all I had room for at the moment. I wasn't thinking about the tour, and I definitely wasn't thinking about what happened that night in Sausalito. (I had spent the last three days trying to wrap my head around that crazy night, then trying to forget it.) So there I was, relaxed and at home, watching the birds and eating my breakfast. I couldn't have been less prepared for what happened next.

I looked at the granola and was ready to scoop up another bite when I noticed something rather strange. The bowl of the spoon was bent at a ninety-degree angle, as if the metal had been melted by a blowtorch when I wasn't looking. I didn't even have enough time to react before the spoon hit the yogurt and slid helpless and empty to the other side of the bowl. It took a second for my mind to catch up and realize what I was looking at. But how? How did a perfectly normal, solid spoon bend without ever leaving my hand? Though it was the first time I asked such a question, it certainly wouldn't be the last.

I sat there for at least a minute looking down at the mangled metal I held. I didn't dare set it down, for fear it would turn out to have been an illusion or would suddenly reshape itself again, returning to its original mundane form. Pushing the chair back, I never looked away from the spoon, just sat there staring with a helpless look on my face.

There were only two possible explanations, I thought to myself. Either I bent the spoon with my own hands without realizing it, which would mean I was more exhausted than I first thought, or it had happened on its own. I didn't want to consider what that meant. It was easier to believe I was crazy or, at best, overworked. I would rather go back to my room and sleep for two days straight than consider the possibility that I bent the spoon with my mind.

A welcomed laugh escaped through my tightened lips and broke the hypnotic spell I had cast. "What a bunch of crazy nonsense," I said, just loud enough to hear. "As if it's possible to bend a spoon with the power of my mind while staring out the window at a few birds." My willingness to even consider that option simply amazed me, and I finally stood up from my chair to get another spoon. Why take a chance, my unconscious mind seemed to say. Maybe it was a defect in the metal itself. The same thing would have happened to anyone in the house if they had picked up that particular piece of silverware. I walked over to the drawer and opened it.

What I did next surprised even me, considering my line of conscious thought. It even scared me a bit.

I reached into the drawer and picked a new spoon, but instead of turning around and walking back to the table where my granola was getting soggy, I paused. My right hand closed the drawer while I held the spoon in my left the same way I held it before. There was no real grip, just a light balancing act between my thumb and first two fingers. I stared down at the spoon with haunted eyes, afraid of the power that might spring forth like a sharp dagger. There were no real thoughts in my mind, just the blank horror of possibility.

Then it happened. A thought began to form, like a cloud born suddenly in a cloudless sky, a thought that didn't seem to come from me but from a place I had never touched before. I had thrown a bucket into a well that didn't seem to have a bottom, and I listened for the distant splash that would prove me wrong. Then I pulled hard on the frayed rope, one hand over the other, until I was able to see what was inside the bucket, the dark, confusing liquid I had stolen from the Earth's core. One word came, more of a feeling than a collection of letters or sounds, but within the womb of that word lived a whole universe I had never known before.

BEND! And it did just that, right there in my hand.

Were my eyes tricking me? Sometimes a spoon, or any straight object for that matter, can appear to bend because of the angle at which it is held or the loose, pulsing rhythm of the wrist making it seem to go rubbery. But these are optical illusions, and I wasn't looking at anything like that. As it had before, the spoon had simply given itself to gravity and bent straight toward the ground. I held the handle in my hand but the rest of it, well, it seemed to have a will of its own and moved without physical aid. It was not the physical part I was concerned about, but the non-physical. I had enough sense to know what hadn't happened; now I needed to find out what had.

I placed the spoon on the counter and took out a fork that was a good deal thicker. Again I held it lightly between my fingers and "felt" the bend. This is the only way I can describe what happened, as if I instinctively knew that the key wasn't what I thought, but what I felt. I felt the joy I would experience if the fork suddenly lost its grip on the solid, lucid universe and bent like a helpless blade of grass. I could sense a growing anxiousness as I waited, as if the weight of this utensil required far more energy than I had used before. The spoon was a good deal lighter and more flexible than the fork, and I decided that this made for a good test. A minute passed and nothing happened. I wasn't disappointed for long.

I could feel the metal that connected the handle to the teeth getting hot, so I rubbed it a little until the heat was too much to bear. Another few seconds passed, and I thought I could see something happening. The metal was moving, and before long the end began its slow dip toward the Earth. It didn't fall nearly as much as the spoon had, but there was a definite change.

Next I tried a butter knife, but no matter how long I focused, it resisted my psychic manipulation. I went back to the spoons, easy prey as I had already discovered, and within two minutes had destroyed three of them. I called to the other room where two of my housemates, Joanne and Sharon, were working. I felt like a child that had been given one of those magic trick kits, "101 Magic Tricks You Can Perform For Your Friends." There was an electricity in the air, and I didn't know if it was just me or if everything around me had changed. Joanne was the first to arrive and asked what was wrong.

"There's nothing wrong. To the contrary," I said to her. "I want to show you something."

I picked up a spoon and held the handle between two fingers. The thumb and index finger of the other hand gently rubbed the thin metal between the bowl and the handle, and Joanne wondered what she was about to see.

"If that spoon bends I'm going to pass out" she said to me. The spoon did bend, farther than it had before, and she nearly kept her promise. I had to hold her arm so she wouldn't crumble.

Sharon came into the kitchen at that same moment. "What's happening?" she asked.

"Oh, nothing," Joanne said sarcastically. "Jimmy just bent a spoon with his mind . . . very ordinary stuff . . . I think I'm going back to bed now."

"Wait . . . one more time," I said to them. And just as easily as that I bent another spoon in front of my stupefied friends. By then seven spoons and a fork sat on the counter bent beyond use. The adventure had certainly begun.

I was all but worn out by the time we arrived at the home in Sausalito for what Sharon called, "An Informal Evening with James Twyman." It was the first real tour Sharon had helped me organize, and to say she was enthused would be an understatement. She had only been working with me for a few months, her chosen retirement after twenty-five years of teaching, and she was already indispensable. I thought she would be able to book maybe ten to twelve events over the course of a month. By the time she was finished, there were twenty-three concert/talks on the January schedule, and the marathon was on.

The "Informal Evening" was her brainchild, and it accounted for maybe five of the twenty-three events that month. She felt that there was no sense having an open evening to rest when there were plenty of people willing to invite forty or fifty people into their homes for a talk. For me it was the chance to relax a bit and not subject myself to the pressures of afternoon sound checks and ticket sales . . . just a room full of people eager to learn. It was a great idea, but by the time we reached San Francisco, I felt the need for a break.

There was no time for that. Sharon had booked three separate events on that particular Sunday throughout the Bay Area, and the "Informal Evening" was the grand finale. In the morning I sang at a Religious Science Church service in Oakland, a primarily African-American congregation that set a powerful and energetic tone for my day. Then I was off to a conference sponsored by a local radio host named Judith Conrad to speak for an hour. Both events were excellent and fun, and by the time evening came I was more ready for a nap than another talk.

We arrived in Sausalito around 6:45 P.M., fifteen minutes before the talk began. It is my habit to be alone before giving a talk, partly because of the need to center myself, but mainly because I need time to figure out what I will say. This applies to large events as much as Sharon's "Informal Evenings" since I have never fallen into the habit of planning ahead. My experience has shown that the less I plan the better the event seems to be. It's hard to say exactly why this is so, but I have always believed that the more I "get out of the way" the more wisdom comes through. That doesn't imply that I'm channeling (except in the highest sense of the word), but rather, who am I to decide in advance what an audience needs to hear? Better to let it happen on its own rather than have me direct the course.

I was walking up and down the street outside the house, watching the cars pull up from a safe distance. One drawback to Sharon's idea is that the average house is not set up for such events; for example, dressing rooms are hard to come by. The choice is to sit quietly in a nine-year-old boy's bedroom, meditating while the crowd files in, or go for a walk. I never felt comfortable displacing children from their sanctuary, even if it's only for a few minutes, so the neighborhood walk was usually my choice.

The coordinators for this particular evening were my friends Will and Grace. They had sponsored many of my Bay Area concerts and workshops over the past two years, and I knew they would get word out in a big way . . . not that it's hard to fill a living room. By the time I decided to return, the house was full and I made my way to the front. Sharon was at the door, checking off names and keeping things organized. She smiled as I walked in, and she motioned with her eyes that she would hold the rear in case anyone walked in late.

I sat down in front of fifty or so people in a living room belonging to someone I had never met, and the event began. It would be impossible to remember what I talked about, and it isn't really important. I remember that the moon was rising in the large picture window just behind me, casting an etheric glow upon the faces of everyone in the room. I remember the way it felt to look into those bright eyes and open faces, knowing that we were there for some important reason, though none of us knew exactly what it was. It was one of those rare evenings when all the pistons fired at once, and the energy between us was amazing.

After an hour, we took a break, and I milled about, introducing myself to the people I had never met, and connecting warmly with those I had. I forgot how tired I was before the talk began in the flow of an evening that had more purpose than I could ever have imagined. There was no way for me to judge what that meant, at least not at that particular moment, but there was a feeling I couldn't describe that seemed to electrify the evening. How could I have known how dead-on that feeling was?

When the break was over the living room filled up again, and I went back to my seat in the front of the group. People were spread out on the floor in front of me, or relaxing into the large oversized couches and chairs against the wall, or lounging somewhere in the back near the door. I could see Sharon sitting dutifully at her table, even though it was well past the hour when latecomers would come sliding in through the back. A typical night in Marin County, the kind of thing that happened all the time in this modern Mecca of sensitive spirituality.

And that's when I noticed him for the first time. He was sitting on the floor in the front row with his hands crossed neatly in front of him. The fact that he had not been sitting there before the break did not interest me as much as the fact that he was there at all. I knew the people on either side of the boy and was certain he did not belong to them. His parents had to be in the room somewhere, but he seemed so alone sitting there, although not at all uncomfortable. He was absorbing every word, or so it seemed, and displayed none of the ten-year-old fidgeting one would expect. His dark hair fell over his eyebrows and barely touched his back collar, and his smile was big and bright. It never seemed to fade as the talk wound on and on. There was something about his eyes, as if they didn't belong to him at all but to a wise old sage displaced from a cave high in the Himalayas. They were deep and mysterious, but no matter what I felt, he was still just a boy, a very attentive young boy, and he immediately fascinated me.

Though I tried to keep my focus, I found myself speaking directly to him, as if he were the only person in the room. My eyes would scan the group but they always ended up locked on him, and it made me feel very comfortable, somehow. His clothes were a bit strange, considering the way everyone else was dressed. His button-up shirt was unpressed and his pants seemed to be a bit too short for his size. The fact that he didn't have any shoes on made no impression at all since this was, after all, Marin County, and shoes are always left at the door. He made the atmosphere seem more surreal than it already was, which, considering everything, was quite a trick.

The talk finally ended and I did what I could to make my way through the crowd to the front door. I wanted to make sure the boy didn't leave before I had the chance to say goodbye, and to ask him . . . I still wasn't sure about that. It didn't really matter what I asked him, I just wanted to look into his eyes again and find out why he was there . . . if I could. I also wanted to find out who his parents were, not that it made a difference, but it seemed to matter somehow. It was so strange, my bizarre interest in a little boy who just happened to be sitting in the front row of one of my talks. It probably was nothing at all, just my runaway imagination. But what if it was more? What if his eyes really did communicate something deep and real, a language normal eyes can never comprehend?

People came up and thanked me for the evening. I tried to be attentive and listen to their words, but they all seemed so far away, like echoes from a dream that I had forgotten and didn't care about. All that mattered was finding that boy, though I had no idea why it was so important to me.

"Hello, thank you for letting me come tonight." The voice came from my left and was accompanied by a light tap on the lower part of my arm. I turned around and saw him standing there, looking up with those penetrating eyes. I also noticed that he spoke with a slight accent, almost Russian or Balkan, definitely Eastern European.

"Oh . . . thank you," I said to him, surprised he was there so suddenly. "I'm glad you liked it . . . though it was a surprise to have someone your age so interested."

"Why?" He asked the question with such innocence, as if he wasn't sure why I asked it at all, as if there was not a reason in the world that he wouldn't be interested in what I had to say. In that instant I knew that there really was something to my feeling, that he wasn't just a figment of my imagination but a true mystery. I looked around again to see if there were any adults looking in our direction, a clue as to who his parents were. No one was looking.

"Well," I finally said, "I guess most young boys your age are more interested in skateboards and video games than talks on spirituality. How old are you, if you don't mind me asking?"

"I'm ten . . . and my name is Marco."

"Thanks Marco, that was my next question."

"So, why aren't most kids interested in God?"

Once again, the openness of his question disarmed me and left me very little room to move. I suddenly realized that I wouldn't be able to water down my answer, or sugarcoat some nice little fairy tale to pacify him. He seemed genuinely confused about the subject and needed a real answer. But what could I say?

"You see, all the children I know are very interested in this," he continued. "We talk about God all the time . . . because it's what we like to talk about."

"Really . . . that's amazing." It was a ridiculous response, but the only one that popped into my head. "Where are you from, Marco?" I asked, trying to change the subject.

"I'm from Bulgaria . . . but I still want to know what you think about children . . . why there are not more here."

It was obvious that I wasn't going to get away, so I sat down in a chair so I could look him in the eye.

"Well, as you see, there are mainly adults here, Marco. I'm not sure why, because when I was a kid, I was a lot like you. I was very interested in God. But I was also very different from most of my friends . . . I'm glad you're not because it sounds like the kids you play with have more in common . . . "

"I didn't mean the kids I play with," he said, with a certain quality I could not define . . . still can't. "I mean the kids I talk to on the inside, the ones who are part of the 'Net.'"

"Do you mean the Internet? Are these the kids you talk to on the computer?"

"I don't have a computer," he said. "I mean on the inside . . . that's where they are, all of them."

He said those words in a way that was both fascinating and frightening. What did he mean by the "inside"? Whatever it was he was talking about, it seemed perfectly normal to him, and so I didn't want to show my surprise. The last thing I wanted was for Marco to get scared.

"I see, the kids you talk to on the inner plane? That makes sense to me. How many kids are there that you communicate with?"

"I don't know," he said. "I guess a lot . . . it changes sometimes . . . like there are more one day and less the next. Some of the kids stop doing it when they get older and others are made to stop."

"What do you mean by that?" I could feel the hair on my arm stand to attention.

"Some people don't want us to talk on the inside, because they're afraid of what it means, I guess. They think we might hurt people . . . but that's not true. We do it to help people, like a good club that does nice things. Do you understand what I mean?"

"Yes, I think I do," I said, lying to him. "But tell me more about the people that don't want you to talk on the inside. Why would they . . ."

"I really don't want to talk about that any more," he said. "I have another question I want to ask you."

"Shoot," I said to him.

"Do you know how to jump inside people's lives and see things about them?"

It was like he hit me in the side of the head with a brick. See inside of people? I was starting to wonder if Marco was putting me on, or if he was a little off balance. I looked over my shoulder hoping that his distraught mother would come save me. She didn't.

"No, I can't say I know how to do that, Marco. What does that mean, jump into people's lives?"

"Sometimes when I'm around people I see a lot of television screens in my mind, and they're all showing something different . . . like different shows, but always about that person. If I want I can jump into one of the screens and see whatever I want. It's sort of like watching a movie, but it's a real movie . . . it's what happened to them a long time ago, sometimes when they were little kids. Some of the kids I talk to on the inside can do it too, and I was wondering if you could."

"Well, that's a question no one has ever asked me before," I said to him. "Let me ask you more. When you do this thing, jump inside people, do you think you're seeing real things, or could it maybe just be imagination?"

"Don't you believe me?"

"Sure I believe you," I said, trying to hide my concern. "It's just that what you're describing is very unusual. Most people can't do that kind of thing."

"I can do it right now if you want," he said, and I could feel the prickly feeling again.

"Really . . . okay, let me see you do it."

He closed his eyes, and, for a moment, I was sure I was being had. After all, his parents probably immersed Marco in all sorts of crazy New-Age philosophy and he had become confused by it all. Why else would he be at a lecture on a Sunday night when he should be home getting ready for school the next day?

"I see you in a garage," he said with his eyes still closed, and an eerie mist seemed to float through the room. "You're crying because your dog is gone . . . he ran away. You've been in there all day crying and won't come out. I think you're about my age, maybe older. Your mother is coming out now and says it's time to come inside for dinner, but you . . ."

"Okay, that's enough," I said, as sweat began forming on my forehead. He was right about everything he saw, and no one knew that story but me. I was twelve years old and our family dog had just run away. He ran away many times but always came back. For some reason I knew that he wasn't coming back this time, and I was right. I sat there in the garage all day . . .

"His name was Hansel . . . your dog."

"That's right, Marco . . . his name was Hansel. That was amazingly accurate. You told the story exactly as it happened."

"Yes . . . like I told you, I see it like a movie."

"Do you know why you have this gift," I asked, "or what you're meant to do with it?"

"It's part of the 'Net,' part of what all the children are doing. Everyone has different things they can do. I can see things, and sometimes move things with my mind."

I was feeling a bit unsteady, as if it was all happening too fast. It's one thing to talk for two hours about this stuff, but to have a little boy come up to you later, a little boy from Bulgaria, and actually do it . . . well, that takes a little getting used to. I was certainly convinced by then that he was real, which made me wonder more about the "Net" he kept talking about.

That was when he asked me the question that changed my life.

"Do you want to be able to do it?"

"I'm sorry, what did you say, Marco?"

"Do you want to be able to see the screens like me? I can give them to you if you want."

How does one answer a question like that? Things were going from weird to weirder, and I was ready to pack my things and leave. But what if he meant what he said, and he really could make me see and do the things that came so natural to him? Part of me wanted to turn away and start a conversation with whoever was nearest, but the other part knew what I would say.

"Of course I do. Can you make me see them?"

"Hold out your finger like this," he said as he stretched his left index finger toward mine. I held out my finger and he touched it with his. That was all.

"Okay, that should do it," he said, looking me straight in the eyes with a happy smile lighting his face.

"That will make me see the screens like you?"

"I think so . . . I've never done it before, so we'll wait and see."

I forgot that I was talking to a child at this point and wanted to get as much out of him as I could. "But how will I know? Will it just happen on its own or will I have to do something?"

"We'll see," he said again. "Adults normally can't do it, but it may be different now. I don't know . . . but the 'Net' is very big and can fit many people."

"Will you tell me more about this 'Net'?" I asked, but before he could answer, a woman grabbed me by the arm and asked me a question about a point I made earlier.

"I just have to ask you," she said in a feverish voice, not at all sensitive to the fact that I was talking to Marco, more than talking, fully engaged. I tried to push that thought away and smiled warmly, giving her permission to continue. "When you met the Emissaries in the mountains of Bosnia . . ." and the question continued for some time.

I spoke with the woman for several minutes, then looked to see where Marco had gone. I searched the living room where a number of people were still gathered, and I looked in the kitchen, but he was nowhere to be found. I decided to stand by the front door and wait, figuring he had gone to find his parents, and these were people I wanted to meet. What kind of people have a kid like Marco, I wondered? Did they even know how special he was? I stood by the door for a long time, saying goodbye to everyone as they left, but Marco never came. He had slipped out when I was talking to the woman, I figured, and now there was no way for me to find out who he was or where I could find him.

A short while later, Sharon and I were driving away toward the hotel. I didn't say anything for a long time, as if I was going to be able to figure out with my mind what had just happened to my soul. But what exactly had happened? Other than an impressive psychic trick, nothing. He touched my finger and nothing happened at all. Was anything supposed to happen? That was impossible to say, since I didn't know what he did, if anything at all. In the end I decided to file the whole thing away under "Strange Children I Have Met," and relax. If I met Marco again, I would find out more. If I didn't . . . well, nothing would be lost.

"I have a question," I asked Sharon as she drove the motor home north on Rt. 101. "Did you get a chance to talk to that little boy? His name was Marco and I had quite a fascinating conversation with him."

I can still hear her response like an echo that never seems to leave my mind. "What boy? There wasn't a little boy there, at least not that I could see, and I was the one welcoming everyone."

"What do you mean?" I asked in a tone that was a bit too direct. "Of course he was there . . . I talked to him for at least ten minutes. And he said things to me that were . . . well, pretty amazing. And then he touched me. Are you really saying that you didn't see a little boy the whole night?"

"There were only about fifty people there, so it would have been hard to miss a boy. There were no children at all, at least not that I saw."

I didn't say another word until we arrived at the hotel. Sharon didn't see him. But how was that possible? I stood there in the middle of the living room talking to him for . . . for quite a while. Everyone must have seen us talking.

But no one did. The next day I asked at least three people if they remembered seeing Marco, but the answer was always the same. "I didn't see any children at all." But he was there, that was all I knew, even if I was the only one who saw him.

Three days later a spoon bent in my hand.

A full day had passed since I discovered my "new talent." In that time I had managed to completely mystify, amaze, and finally annoy the people I lived and worked with. It's funny how little time it takes for a fantastic skill like bending spoons with one's mind to become completely ordinary. Do it the first five times, and it's a miracle. Twenty times later, it's like a mutant curse. I was ordered, rightfully so, to replace all the silverware I had bent, and by then the number was substantial. I also noticed a certain look in their eyes when they saw me standing near the drawer where we kept the utensils. If they were lucky enough to see me before I saw them, they would turn around and act like they had forgotten something in the office or in the other room. Such was the terrible psychic disease that had befallen me.

But I had only discovered the tip of the iceberg. There was still so much life beneath the water waiting to spring to the surface and breathe. It got to the point where it was hard to get any real work done in the house. I became obsessed with seeing how far I could push this skill, and how far past spoon bending it would go. I began a series of experiments, and it didn't matter who helped me. Whoever happened to be standing around without their nose buried in a computer screen was fair game. I quickly realized that I was developing the ability to read thoughts, but only to a limited degree. My experiments included sending thoughts as well as receiving them, and the success rate in both was amazing.

The house where I lived and worked—Casa De Paz was the name we gave it—teemed with activity day and night. It was hard for our little community, five people total, to find space to be alone and think. Sharon lived in an RV parked in the driveway, another of her "retirement passions," Joanne and Drayton lived together in the master bedroom, and Stephanie had the room in the back beside my own. It was probably one of the largest and nicest houses in Joshua Tree, the tiny town bordering the national park in California's high desert, a forty-minute drive from Palm Springs. I had moved there a year and a half earlier, primarily because of my friendship with Joanne, and together we started an interesting little business, though I use the word "business" loosely. People all over the world had asked me to design an Internet study course that would take the lessons I learned from the Emissaries of Light in the mountains of Bosnia to a deeper level. We called it "The Beloved Community," and by the time I met Marco there were more than six hundred people involved. It was a full-time job for everyone at the house, so it was no wonder everyone lost interest in my "experiments" very quickly.

It is hard for me to remember those first few days, even though I am writing this book only a few months later. It was like

15

being thrown into an ocean I had never seen before, an ocean so vast and pure, more beautiful than anything I had ever experienced. All I wanted to do was explore this grand new place and see what treasures it would reveal. Every experiment I conducted seemed to ground the gift deeper into my soul. Was this what Marco intended to do to me? He said he had never tried to give it away before, but he did, all by simply touching my index finger. He didn't know if it would work or not, but it certainly had worked. The spoons in the trash proved that. And now there was more, much more, and I had no idea where it would end.

I was also obsessed with finding the boy again. I called everyone I could think of in the Bay Area, especially those who were at the evening talk where we met, but no one reported seeing Marco, let alone knowing who he was. There were no Bulgarian children running around, jumping into people's lives as far as they knew. But what did they know? Marco was no dream or illusion. He was a real flesh-and-bone kid I had met and touched. We must have stood there talking for ten minutes with people all around us. Either everyone in that room was blind except for me, or something happened that no one could explain.

I didn't want to explain it. I was having too much fun, the sort of fun I used to have when I was in high school doing magic tricks for my friends. There was something about that feeling of knowing something that no one else knew, or being able to do something that seemed impossible. The only difference was that I was only doing tricks in high school, but this was real. If I had wanted to I could have broken the first rule everyone learns in "Magic 101" and told everyone in high school how I did it. Of course, then the mystery would be gone and they wouldn't appreciate it nearly as much. People only think they want to know how a trick works, but they really don't. But this was so very different because I couldn't have explained it if I wanted to. There was nothing up my sleeves and no white rabbit hidden beneath my jacket. It was something beyond magic, beyond tricks, something very, very real.

Sharon was my favorite subject, or guinea pig, as I liked to call her. One day I sat her down and gave her a stack of five index cards and a pencil. I sat on the other side of the table with a similar pile. I had no idea what I was going to ask her, only that I would come up with a random set of questions and have her write the answers down on the cards.

"Write down the name of your first dog, your pet when you were a kid," I said to her. She concentrated for a moment and wrote something on the card, then set it face down on the table. I then opened up my mind and waited for an image. At first nothing came, but I began to feel something, as if I could sense the presence of a small dog to my left looking up at me. I closed my eyes and tried to focus on the feeling. Then I saw, if seeing is the right word, a scruffy terrier with wide-open eyes, panting as if we were sitting beneath the kitchen table, and it hoped to be the beneficiary of an accidental drop. I looked at the dog in my mind and asked it what its name was. I would love to say that the dog spoke to me, like one of those commercials where dogs and cats move their mouths like real people when no one is looking; but it wouldn't be true. But a name began to form, like an airplane writing letters in the sky, one by one. I waited until all the letters formed and I could see the name. I wrote the word Buffy on my card. "Scruffy Buffy"—what a perfect name.

I repeated the same experiment three more times with different random questions. I asked her for the street number of her house when she was a child, the name of her favorite book, and the name of her favorite song. I followed the same order as before, having her write down her answer, then after focusing my mind trying to duplicate it on my own card. It seemed to be getting easier each time, though we would have to wait until the end to see how accurate I was.

"Now I want you to write down the name of the town where you were born." Sharon concentrated and wrote something on the last card, then laid it face down on top of the others.

I felt a slight pressure in my temples as I began to focus again. Sharon held the name of the town in her mind and I tried to throw out the line and reel it in. Once again, I saw the airplane writing letters in the sky, but as each letter formed, the pressure increased until it was more of a dull pain. I tried to ignore it and held the image of the letters and the sky; just a couple more and I would see the word. Seconds later my temples throbbed in agonizing waves of white heat, and the world began to turn a thick gray. Then I could see it, VERNONIA. I wrote the word on my card and then collapsed backward in my chair.

"What's wrong?" Sharon asked me.

"I suddenly have the worst headache of my life, like a train just cracked my skull open."

"Was it there before, or is it because of the experiment?"

"I don't know . . . I mean, no it wasn't there before. I felt fine when we started. Do you think there's a connection, like these things I'm doing are giving me . . ." I didn't want to say it, didn't want to even think about it. "It's probably just the heat . . . you know the desert."

"Jimmy, it's only February," Sharon said as she put the back of her hand on my forehead, checking to see if I had a fever. "Maybe you should stop for a while . . . give up these experiments. You've already proven you can . . ."

"I can't stop," I nearly shouted at her as I bolted up. "It won't let me stop. There's something inside that's pushing me to see how far it can go, how powerful this gift can be. I don't know why but I have to keep going, even if my head splits in two."

"It might," she said. "It might do just that. You don't know why this happened or what it's all about. Marco did something, or triggered something in you . . . I believe that. But you don't know why he did it. You've become obsessed with the whole thing, as if nothing else is important to you. Your little Internet school is suffering, your friends are worried about you, all so you can read minds and bend spoons."

"Speaking of that, let's turn over our cards and see how I did." We turned them over one at a time, and the results were stunning. I had four out of five perfect, and the fifth, the question about her favorite book, was very close. I don't know what that proved because the pain in my head was still cutting me in half, but at least the skill was progressing. At that moment it was all that mattered to me.

There are doors within us so used to being closed that, when they finally open, the screech is enough to wake the dead. The hinges in certain areas of our minds are dry from disuse and need oil, but if we neglect them, then we suffer from the noise when the seal of rust has been broken, and we think we're being snapped in two. But the door must be opened, with or without the oil, for we cannot progress down that road until we've searched every room in that large house. Perhaps we're afraid of what we might find, or discover more power than we know how to use, and so the doors remain bolted, never once feeling the fresh movement of air and light. The house grows stale and cold, and no one visits us anymore, until the day a tornado comes that rattles the walls and forces the door to swing wide. Everything is revealed and there are no more illusions about what is and what is not. It is a good thing to happen, but the noise, yes the noise, can be so terrible.

My obsession to see how far I could push my psychic powers continued, and so did the headaches. If I only pushed a little, bent one or two spoons or conducted one experiment, then the pain was not too great, and I could move on with the more important events of my day. But I was like an alcoholic in a brewery, and I wasn't able to slow the course of the powerful river rushing through my mind. *Just one more experiment or one more piece of metal, then I will stop.* But I never did. By noon my head was pounding so hard that I could hardly move, and it was the only thing that made me stop for a while. *Rest until the pain becomes bearable, then start again. Keep pushing until you can't push any more, then you'll know the truth, you'll know what this gift is really for.* But it was getting to be too much, and even then, I wasn't sure how much further I could push myself.

What had he done to me, the boy that no one saw? It was as if he planted a seed in my head that was growing larger every minute, every time I pushed the gift to see how far it would go. How much room was left inside my head? Would the seed grow until it took over every inch of space, leaving no room at all for my own thoughts and my own mind? What if he wasn't a little boy at all, but something much darker, much more sinister? If only I could stop the experiments, stop pushing to see . . . whatever it was I wanted to see. I didn't even know, only that I had no control over myself, and whether I wanted to or not, I wasn't going to stop, until . . . until *It* happened. What *It* was I still had no idea, but I knew it was there, waiting for me.

I had fallen into a deep well, and no one was able to pull me out. A week after the whole thing started, I was in my room with bent spoons covering the bed. Looking back now, I see that it is a wonder my friends didn't have me committed. Perhaps they were afraid of what I was becoming, or what I would do to them if they tried to make me stop. Even I couldn't ignore their concern, or the long, hard looks they gave me whenever I approached them with one of my "new experiments." Even Sharon, who until then had been my strongest supporter, refused to help me. But, at that point, it didn't really matter. I was turning into a different person, someone I didn't recognize, and I didn't know how to make it stop, nor did I want to.

After about two weeks, I was scheduled to give a couple of talks, one in Palm Springs and the other in Anchorage, Alaska, and I knew it was time to leave my tomb. I have had friends who were bipolar, and I had the opportunity to be around one of them when he was neck deep in an "episode." It was a frightening experience, and I started to wonder if this is what it was like to be around me. It would have been easy to write the whole thing off to a psychological disorder, but it was really the opposite. Something had fallen into place, not out of place, and I was simply having a difficult time adjusting to the new rhythm. The thought occurred to me that the talks would be an opportunity to practice the "Gift" (for that is really what it seemed to be) in front of an audience. Everyone at the house was dead set against this idea, but by then I was far too gone to listen to their concerns. *Why not make this public, this whole, huge thing that was swimming through my mind? Show people what they're capable of. Make them see the marvels I can perform.* My mind was made up, and I set off on a course that no one could navigate.

I had been a regular speaker at the "The Prophet's Conference," an enormous gathering of people from around the world interested in everything from the power of prayer to UFOs, and I was overjoyed to participate in one so close to my home. I certainly wasn't ready to travel, and even I knew that. The headaches were nearly constant, and I was afraid of what it would be like 35,000 feet in the air. Joanne said that I might blow the plane up if it got too uncomfortable, and though she was surely joking, it occurred to me as a definite possibility. But Palm Springs was only a forty-five-minute drive from Joshua Tree, and I was confident that I could survive the trip. A thousand people would be there, the perfect opportunity for me to "come out."

The conference was already humming by the time I arrived, head throbbing and body still adjusting to being away from the house. I didn't realize it would be so hard to be around people again. I skated around the crowd for a minute or two, staying to the fringe so no one would recognize me. There was something very wrong with me, and I sensed a faint recognition of this fact, but the temptation to show off the gift Marco gave me was too great to withstand. Somewhere inside my head, the voice of reason was still alive, and now and then I could even tell it apart from all the other clanging sounds, but for the most part, it was a distant echo that faded before those stronger forces. They rose above my head like enormous waves that sent my body cascading toward the ocean floor. I tried and tried to withstand the force but its hold over me was still too strong.

Give into it . . . let it show you the wonders of psychic power. Why are you trying to fight what you know is stronger than you? Don't listen to those others . . . they don't have any way of knowing what this means, or what you could do. How could they unless they felt the wings of destiny brush against their faces as you have? How can they understand any of it, no matter how much they think they can. Run away . . . do what you want with it. In the end you're the one who will have the power, you're the one who will win.

I checked into my room and lay down on the bed, hoping to ease the pain that was already more than I could comfortably handle. I had not done any experiments that day, hoping to regain my strength for the conference, but I had been pushing so hard until then, and no matter how many aspirin I took, the pain never left. The shades were pulled and the lights were off, but still there was no relief. Finally, gratefully, I dozed off to sleep, and at least for a while the pain was gone.

The people had left the house and I was alone. I had been looking forward to the evening talk in Sausalito for weeks, but it had been a disaster. "Why did I say those things?" I kept muttering to myself. "Why did you have to keep pushing it . . . pushing it to the point that they started to hate you?" There was a faint memory of what I had done, but it was so vague and unclear that it didn't even matter. All that did matter was that they were gone, and I was standing in the middle of the living room wondering why.

The refreshment table had hardly been touched. I must have said something terrible before the break for them to leave like that, for the table, set so beautifully, to be undisturbed. I walked over and poured a cup of coffee into the white paper cup, then looked around for the sugar. There it was, right next to the spinach dip, so perfect in its glass bowl. There was moisture on the outside of the bowl of dip, which meant it probably hadn't been there very long. It had been set there minutes before I cleared the room with whatever it was I said or did . . . God knows I didn't have any idea what it was. I picked up the sugar bowl, then looked around for the spoons. They were hidden behind the chips, but there was something very wrong. The spoons were set inside a large plastic cup, the kind of hard plastic that should be stable, but every one of them was bent and twisted beyond recognition. There was no way to bend them back in place, and nothing else to stir the coffee with. I took a pen that was lying nearby, wiped it off on my pant leg and put it in my cup. The coffee mixed and I took a sip. Nothing else was right at all.

I walked around the house hoping to find someone, anyone, that remained. Maybe someone was in the bathroom when the disaster struck and would come out any minute, wondering what had happened. They would look at me as if I was supposed to know, and I was, but I didn't. Then they would grab their coat and leave like the rest, figuring I had done something awful to cause such an exodus. I had done something terrible, and the house was as quiet as a cemetery. I was afraid to make any sound myself.

Then I heard someone coming up the stairs from the basement, light steps that didn't sound quite right. I slipped behind the kitchen door and waited to see who it was. The steps were so slow and deliberate, like someone who was in no hurry at all, certainly not someone who was trying to leave fast. They were near the top of the stairs now and I looked out to see who it was. All I could see was the back of someone's head, a boy's head. He slowly turned around, and I saw who it was. Marco.

It all came back to me, not the terrible deed that cleared the room, but the whole story with Marco. I remembered meeting him in this very same room, talking to him and hearing all sorts of odd stories, things I didn't expect from any ten-year-old boy. He said he could do fantastic things like see into people's lives, and I didn't believe him at first. But then he touched my finger and a few days later my world turned upside down. And there he was looking at me with a child's smile, looking as if nothing had happened at all.

"Hi," he said as he stood there at the top of the stairs.

"Hi back," I said to him.

"Are you mad at me?" There was suddenly a hurt look on his face, like a child who was afraid he had done something wrong and was about to get punished.

"No, I'm not mad at you," I said, "just confused."

"Why are you confused?"

I walked out of the kitchen until I was sitting down in a chair right in front of Marco. Once again we were face to face. "Well, I meet you, go home, and everything goes to hell. The only problem is that I like what is happening, even though it's ripping my life into shreds. I can't stop it, no matter how I feel. Spoons bend around me, I can read everyone's mind, and life is suddenly a mess. I used to think that this kind of thing would be wonderful, like setting the mind free. But it hasn't been that way at all. If it goes any further, I'll probably self-destruct."

"But why is it my fault?"

"Because you're the one that did it to me. You touched my finger and even though I didn't feel anything then, a few days later, BLAM."

"I didn't think it would be that strong," he said, with a sorry look in his eyes. "I just wanted you to see how I see. That's all."

"Well, it worked, but I think I need something more. How are you able to control the Gift? I can't seem to get my head around it, as if I'm addicted to the whole feeling, to everything I feel when I use it. I love doing it, don't get me wrong, but it destroys my head. Does your head ever feel like it's going to explode after you've done these things?"

"No."

"Mine does, and now the headache doesn't seem to go away. And I think I'm going insane. You've got to help me, Marco. I don't know how, but you need to do something. Maybe you can touch my finger again and make it all go away."

I couldn't believe I was asking him that. Getting rid of the Gift was the last thing on my mind. If anything, I wanted to push it further, as far as I possibly could push it, and who knows where that would lead. Maybe I would become a great healer like Jesus, or maybe more. Maybe there was no limit to what I could do, if I only . . .

"Do you want to know why it hurts so bad?" Marco asked me. I nodded my head. "Because you're using it wrong, completely wrong. You think that the Gift is about psychic powers, but it really isn't. The Gift is about love. The other things just sort of show up by themselves, but they aren't really very important. What is important is that you learn how to love people, and then you'll be able to use the powers for good things, not just to impress people."

"But I'm not trying to impress people." He knew I was lying. I could see it in his eyes. And I knew what he was saying, and that he was right. How had I gotten so sucked into the dramatics of reading minds and bending spoons? I wanted to see how far I could push the Gift just so people would look at me and say, "There goes that amazing psychic dude . . . you better stay away from him or he might turn you into a toad." And I liked that feeling, that power. It meant people would respect me, and even be afraid of me. But no matter how far it went and how much I was able to do, it had nothing to do with love, and I knew it.

"You need to ask yourself this question," he said to me. "What do you really want? Do you want to be able to do really interesting things that look really cool? Or is there something more, something higher? The Gift will give you whatever you want, but you'll also feel the result of what you ask for. If you use it just to impress people, then you're going to feel bad when you're done. But if you use it to help people, then you'll feel that as well."

"How do I use it to help people?" I asked him.

"You decide that's what you want to do, and the Gift shows you how."

"Are the psychic powers bad? Are you telling me I shouldn't be using them?"

"No, I like them too, but they're not the goal. Love is the goal, and sometimes you can use the Gift, or the powers, to bring that to you. But if you misuse it, well, then you won't feel love, but something much darker."

"Like the headache."

"The headache is just the beginning," he said in a very serious tone. "If you use it to become powerful, then you're going to have some big problems. You have to decide what you want, then let the Gift give it to you."

"Why did you give this to me, anyway?" I asked him.

"You're going to find out, but I can't tell you right now."

"Why not?"

"Because it's not time yet. But you do need to make the decision, because none of it will happen if you don't. All I can tell you right now is that we have a message for people, and you need to find it, then tell people that message."

"Who is we?" I asked Marco. "Are there more people who can do this?"

"Yes, many more, and they're children . . . the Children of Oz— that's what they call us. The children who have the Gift have a message that will help people, and that's why I gave it to you."

There was a knock on the door and I sat up in my bed. I sensed that there was something I needed to remember about the dream

I just had, but it seemed to drift away from me so fast that I couldn't quite get ahold of it. I stood up and walked over to the door.

"Joanne, come in, what are you doing here?"

"I came to hear your talk, silly." She came in the room and sat down on the bed. "So, what are you going to do? Just talk and sing?"

I knew what she was really asking me. She wanted to know if I was going to do any of my demonstrations for the crowd. I had fully intended to, but suddenly, for no apparent reason at all, I felt like I didn't want to, as if it wasn't important.

"No, I mean yes, I'm just going to talk and sing. None of the exciting stuff tonight. Besides, my head is still killing me."

"Good," she said as she stood up from the bed. "I mean, good that you're not going to do any of that scary stuff, not that your head hurts."

And that was it. Something had changed between the time I laid my head down and when I woke up from my nap. There was something about that dream, though I still did not remember what it was. It didn't come back to me for quite some time.

It was a stifling hot day in Palm Springs, which is to say that the sidewalk was as hot as a skillet with three eggs frying on top, and the wind felt like a fan blowing in front of a furnace. Those who came to attend the Prophet's Conference from milder climates may have heard rumors of the harsh oppression that this town dishes out like gravy, but to feel it is something else entirely. People got out of their nice air-conditioned cars after driving from San Diego or Los Angeles, or stepped off their commuter flights at the Palm Springs airport, only to be confronted with the stark reality of life in the California desert. Summer was still several months away, but the heat was already upon them. "Come back in August for some real fun," the locals would say. "Only the scorpions and lizards have hide enough for that sort of heat, surely not tourists coming in for a weekend conference. Best be long gone by then if you want to breathe."

Of all the conferences I've had the honor to present at, this was my favorite. It was the fourth time my name was listed beside such speakers as Jean Houston, Edgar Mitchell, Gregg Braden, and Hank Wessleman. It was like a New-Age traveling circus—pull into town and set up shop, fly through the air and leave the audience begging for more. The fact that I was included at all was a great honor, and I hope I showed my gratitude by offering an inspired thought or two. Add what you can and smile at everyone you meet—that was my motto. But most of all, don't take yourself too seriously, because that was like the kiss of death. Whatever magic was present before would be lost in the soup of egotism, and it would be the last invitation I would receive. Thank God, then, I had the dream, though it was still an unconscious echo in my mind.

I made my way to the bottom floor of the hotel where the masses were waiting and where the booths were set up like a spiritual shopping mall, table after table of trinkets and remedies, books and CDs. The party was in full swing, and I was ready to go.

I went through the preliminary sound checks and ironed out potential tech glitches in advance, just minutes before my talk was ready to begin. The crowd filed back into the huge hall from the shopping area, and I made my way to a back room to prepare. I was grateful that the headache had reduced to a dull roar, and I was sure to forget it when I stepped onto the stage.

Announcements were made, and the room settled in for yet another talk. It was my turn to stand before them and deliver, but what I was going to say was a mystery even to me. My preoccupation with the recent developments of my life weighed heavily on my mind, leaving very little room for anything else. And now I had decided to leave that line of delivery behind, and my smarter self said it was a good decision. That left me with the "standard" presentation I had performed hundreds of times before, all about the great message of the Emissaries of Light I described in my first book. It was a good talk, but it had none of the zest I felt from my latest adventure. Shift the car into a familiar gear and hit the accelerator. The rest would hopefully take care of itself.

I stood at the side of the risers that served as a stage while I was being announced. Sweat was pouring down my face and I could feel my temples beginning to pound. "Not now," I said just beneath my breath. It just wasn't a good time to have an episode; I felt like an epileptic sensing the approach of a seizure and trying not to fall over and convulse. *Hold it back. Don't give in to it. You can control this thing.* But the tiger already had me by the leg and I didn't think I had enough strength to shake free. Its teeth sank deep into my flesh, and they were like fishhooks that needed pliers to break.

I could hear the applause of the audience as if it was far away. I mounted the steps and took my place in front of the microphone, then took a deep breath. I opened my mouth and let out a long sigh before I was finally ready to begin.

"Thank you, everyone. It's such an honor to be here with you today."

And with that I launched into another talk, sang a few songs and pried the lid of my life back like a can of sardines. I didn't realize the can was so full, and the words came spilling out all over the stage. I started to feel the strength coming back, even though the headache seemed to increase its assault. It was hard to tell which was more powerful, the pain or the sudden flash of energy I felt. I hopped on top of them both like a surfboard and tried to ride the fierce waves. Somehow, in spite of the furious ride, I was able to stay afloat and tune myself to the pulsing rhythm. I could feel the pain, and I could feel the waves beneath my feet, but none of that seemed to matter. I drew my life from the energy of the crowd and was spiraling higher with each word.

Then something happened that I have never experienced before and hope I never will again. As I was talking, I noticed a woman walking from the audience toward the stage. She walked to the right side where there were five steps that led up to the platform where I stood, paused, then mounted the steps. She stood there for a moment with a lost look in her eye, and I thought maybe she had come to fill my water glass. Looking back, I see that it was a strange and far-fetched conclusion, but nothing else seemed logical. Why else would she be standing ten feet from my side in the middle of my lecture? The other possibilities were too scary to consider at that moment.

But then it happened. The temptation was too great, and I stopped in the middle of a sentence and looked straight at her. She looked like a child that was lost in a huge unforgiving crowd and had no idea where her parents had gone. Her eyes widened as I looked at her, and then her mouth opened as if in slow motion. It was as if I was watching a film, completely uninvolved, as if I could reach over, take the remote control and change the channel if I wanted to. If it hadn't happened so fast, perhaps I would have known what to do, but the lightning flash of energy that shot from her nearly knocked me off the stage.

The scream was so shocking that it sent waves of unrelenting fear through the whole room. I took a step backwards as if her scream was a gun ready to send me to the floor, and the sound continued until her lungs were finally empty. Then she drew in another giant breath and started again, her mouth opening like a cave bellowing out its cold, stale clouds of darkness. She screamed until the air was spent, then started over. Over and over the screams came, and no one in the audience moved. No one came onto the stage to help me, no one came to help her back to her seat; everyone was just sitting there watching as if this was part of the script.

It went on for at least three minutes before anything happened. I found my feet and slowly walked toward her. It was only then that I realized how strong the headache had become, and I nearly fell over when I took my first step. I balanced myself and made my way to where the woman stood, her mouth still open wide with pulsing waves of sound rocketing toward me. I wrapped my arms around her as if they were wings, and then she was completely enclosed. But the scream continued, muffled by my shoulder where her face was buried.

It was enough to break the spell she had cast over the audience, and two or three people finally came to our aid. They came up the steps and took her away from me, wrapping themselves like blankets around her body, and leading her down the steps to the floor. Once there, the woman collapsed on her back and her screams became a pitiful whimpering mixed with an occasional moan. I was still standing where they left me, and it was only then that I remembered where I was, and that there were a thousand people watching this strange scene. I turned back toward the microphone and waited another moment before finally opening my mouth.

"This is real," I said to them, "not theoretical. It's one thing to talk about peace at a conference of believers, but it's another thing to bring it out to the world where unexpected things happen, things like what we all just saw." *Why is my head pounding so hard?* "When we're at an event like this it's not hard to find people who will agree with us about these things, but when you walk out that door, that's when the workshop really begins." *Please, make it stop . . . I don't think I can continue like this.* "Different people will react to love in different ways, but it is our job to give only love no matter how it is perceived or received. As *A Course in Miracles* says, 'Everything we ever do is either an act of love or a call for love; therefore, the only proper response in any situation is to give love.' And that's the only real lesson I can offer here today, or learn." *Stop now or you're going to pass out on the stage. STOP NOW.* "So with that, I leave you with the love you never lost, and which has never been compromised. Have a great conference, everyone."

Applause rose from the crowd, and I tried to make my way off the stage without anyone realizing that I was in pain, more than that, that I was nearly ready to die. I knew that whatever happened to that woman had something to do with my headache, and with the Gift. She reacted somehow to what was moving through me, or what was happening to me. I didn't really know what it was, only that I wanted it to stop. The fantastic experience that started off so innocently was tearing my mind apart, and I didn't want it anymore. But how would I make it go away? How would I make it all end before it did the same to me?

A week later, I was in Anchorage and a nearly identical situation occurred while I was on stage. And as before, the event was marked by an increase in the pain in my head, and the sudden feeling that I was transmitting something beyond my conscious mind. A signal of some kind was being released, and people were having very different reactions. But what did it all mean? Was it another strange aspect to the Gift I was given by Marco, or was it something far darker? All I knew at that moment was that everything had changed and I couldn't go around acting as if I didn't know that. Whatever was happening, I had no real control of it, and if it increased in this new terrible direction, then I was certainly lost.

The headaches had become almost unbearable. I spent hours every day curled up on my bed, trying to sleep, for it was the only way I could escape the constant beating of horse hoofs on my broken skull. I stopped the experiments completely, hoping it would slow the assault, but it had already gone too far. Something had to change or I was going to go insane, if I hadn't already.

CHAPTER TWO

A STRANGER IN A STRANGE LAND

Very little changed in the next three months, except that the headaches became decreasingly oppressive, as long as I didn't push my brain with too many experiments. Each morning, I woke up from what seemed like a black void, no dreams, such an unusual experience for me. In the past, much of my inspiration had been drawn from what I called "Night School." It turned out that the dreams hadn't actually stopped at all, and when I came to the end of this strange drama (or at least what seemed like the end), all those dreams returned to my conscious mind like water breaking over a floodgate. There are two in particular that I want to relate, dreams I did not remember until late May 2001, but which had dramatic significance as the story unfolded. They were setting the stage for the adventure that lay ahead, an adventure that had hardly even begun. If I had known what lay ahead I might not have moved at all, but might have lain there in my bed another month or two until the whole thing passed. Thank God I moved, for, as it turned out, my life depended upon it.

Dream #1

I was walking through an eastern European street with Marco, probably in Bulgaria. It was a cool day and people walked with their jackets pulled tightly around their necks, and dark clouds covered the sun, threatening rain. It all seemed perfectly natural, walking there with him in that faraway place. I had been to Sofia, the capital of Bulgaria, once before, and I thought I recognized some of the buildings and sights. But former communist countries have a certain look that makes it hard to tell one from the other, that drab, black-and-white look like brown decay and crumbling cement. None of it seemed out of place in the dream, as if I had been there for a very long time. And it didn't seem unusual that I was there with him, Marco, the boy who started this strange story by holding out his index finger.

"Why do you think this is happening?" he asked me as we stopped at an intersection.

"I'm not sure," I said, "maybe because it's the right time, or we're ready for a new level . . . or even evolution. That's my guess, it's all about evolution. Whenever it's time for a species to break free from the restraints of the old form, a group comes along to mirror that new level, showing the way to live in the new world. Maybe that's why you came to me in the first place."

"I don't even understand what you're saying . . . too complicated for me. But I think you're right, at least I feel like you are. Who is this new group?"

"The Children of Oz," I said as the light turned green and we started across the street. "You're the one who told me about them, the other children who have these gifts. I believe that they're showing the rest of us who we can become."

"Or who we already are," he said.

"Why do you say that?"

"We're no different from you or anyone else," Marco said as he stopped and looked me straight in the eyes. "Just because we can do these things doesn't mean we're higher than you, or more advanced. It's already inside you. I didn't give you anything when I touched your finger. I just helped unlock the door, and then the Gift sort of flew out. So these children are simply showing you who you already are, and offering a kind of key."

"The key that will help everyone open those doors?"

"Yes. Most people are very afraid and they lock the door very tight, wondering what is wrong with them. They need something to help them relax and realize there's nothing out there trying to hurt them. What do you think that is?"

"You mean, what do they need?" I asked.

"Yes."

"Love. I believe we're all looking for the same thing, and love is the only thing we need."

"And love will unlock the door that fear has bolted shut?"

"Yes, that's what I believe," I said to him.

We came to a small park with a small fountain in the middle. Around the fountain there was a circular sidewalk with benches set ten feet apart. Marco and I sat down on one of the benches, and the conversation continued.

"Do you know what an Emissary of Love is, Marco?" I asked him.

"No. What is an Emissary?"

"Well, it's someone who brings or carries something," I said. "So an Emissary of Love is someone who carries love to others. Would you say that the Children of Oz are Emissaries of Love? Is that their real mission, to carry love to humanity?"

He looked around as if he was searching for a good answer. Across from us a woman was holding a baby, smiling at the child and bouncing it up and down on her knee.

"Look at that baby for a minute," he said, not like a ten-year-old, but as if he was the wisest adult I had ever met. "The baby can't do much for herself, just smile and laugh when her mother holds her. But she responds to love, responds to it because it is already inside her. She doesn't need to talk about it or explain it, but who doesn't feel love when they look into the eyes of a baby? Adults are the same way. They usually use their heads and try to explain things, but it's the heart that really communicates. You may build walls around your heart, but given enough love those walls come down, and then you're no different from that baby. That's what we're here for, to help dissolve those walls."

"So we already have what we need, we just need to find it."

"Yes. There's no one out there that can give you anything, but some people can help you unlock certain doors. That's what the children are all about, especially the psychic children. The

Children of Oz are born with the doors taken right off the hinges, and so there's nothing to get in the way of the love coming through. And as they give that love, then they help others do the same."

"But what about the psychic gifts?" I asked. "Why do these children have these powers?"

"I don't really know," he said, then looked away. "I guess it's just how it works. But like I told you before, if you put too much focus on the powers, then they go away."

"Why?"

"Because the powers are there because of the love, and if you forget the love then the powers disappear. Do you understand?"

"I think so, and I seem to have some experience in this. What about the headaches?"

"That's a question you'll have to answer for yourself," he said. "I think that when you answer the real question, then the headaches will simply go away."

"The real question?"

"Yes, that's what you should be looking for."

Dream #2

The next night, the dream picked up right where it left off. We were still sitting in the park with the fountain and the mother, who was by then pushing a stroller with her baby wrapped inside. As before, there was no perceived break in the pattern, as if no time had passed at all. We had simply taken a breath, and then continued our conversation.

"You said something before about the children joining together for some higher purpose," I said to Marco. "What did you mean by that? Are you saying that you're aware of all the other children in the world that have the Gift?"

"In a way, yes, but not in the way you may think. First of all, we're aware of the truth, that we are one, and so we are aware of that oneness. And within that experience we are aware of each other, all the children who have been seeded for this particular purpose."

"Why do you say 'seeded'?" I asked. "That's a very powerful word because it means you were planted here, maybe from some other dimension or planet. Is that true?"

"Don't you think you were planted here?"

"Me? Well, I've never thought about it that way before."

"Haven't you ever had the feeling that you're here to accomplish something?" he asked me. "Don't you get the sense that there's a great shift happening and you came here to be part of it?"

"Actually, yes, I do feel that way," I said to Marco. "So it was a conscious choice on my part, on all of our parts? We're here on the planet at this time because we made that choice?"

"Doesn't it make sense?" he asked, and once again I forgot I was talking to a ten-year-old boy. "Don't you feel it deep inside you, the sense of purpose or mission? It may not have been conscious, but it certainly was intentional."

"Conscious and intentional . . . to me they're the same thing."

"Maybe they are, but these are ultimately just concepts, and the truth is not a concept at all. The truth is a real vibrating thing. So to answer your question, we were all planted here to do something amazing, to be Emissaries of Love like you said before. The psychic children, or the Children of Oz, have a very important role to play in that unfolding. You have your role and we have ours."

"And what exactly is your role?" I asked.

"To simply ask a question."

"A question? What kind of a question?" By then I was too intrigued to stop. He had me, and I wasn't going to let go.

"It's a question that everyone in this world needs to ask themselves. Once they do, then it requires an action of some kind. Our role is to first of all *be* that question, then offer the world a way of answering it themselves."

I looked into his eyes, hoping he would ask me. I didn't want to say the words for some reason. I wanted him to give it to me without asking. My eyes alone said more than words.

"So, you want to hear the question?" he finally said with a smile.

"Yes," I said. "I thought you would never ask."

"Just remember that this is a question you must live, and life will lead you into the answer. If you adopt that attitude, then it won't be a question for long."

I took a deep breath as if this would be a monumental experience for me. Whatever he was about to say or ask, it was the whole mission of the Children of Oz. I had no real way of understanding what that meant, and to this day I am grappling with that. But the moment was so real, so vivid, that I know this was more than an ordinary dream, but rather the way Marco had chosen to communicate these deeper lessons. I sat up straight on the bench and waited.

"I'm going to use your words and ask the question in a way that will make sense to you," Marco said to me. "Here it is: 'How would you act or behave if you knew that you are an Emissary of Love this moment? Begin!' What would you do right now if that were so? How would you act toward everyone you meet? What would you say to them? How would you live your life? You see, that's the only question worth asking right now because it's the real activation point. It's the place where life begins, when you realize that the question is true, that you actually are an Emissary of Love right now. Will you begin, then, or wait for something more?"

"Will I realize that I'm an Emissary of Love right now?" I asked.

"Yes, that's it. That's the mission of the psychic children, to live that answer. I said before that everyone has this within them, but it is normally hidden beneath layers of fear. But if we can hold this frequency, and the world can see us holding it, then it offers a path to a new world."

"So, you want us all to see that the question is true, that we are Emissaries of Love. And when we act from the place of that truth, then it becomes activated within us. Is that correct?"

"You can't *live* it until you *know* it," he said. "You asked me before if we're aware of one another, all the other Children of Oz. The answer is obviously yes. We are working together to establish a kind of net over the whole world that will help people live this truth. I said that we were 'seeded' here, and I meant that too. We're here on purpose, and we're aware of that. It's hard to really explain it well, but if you look into your heart you'll know that it's true, because it's true about you as well."

"Can you tell me more about this net?" I asked him.

"You will learn about it yourself. It's not something that can be explained, only lived. You will live it, I guarantee it. Your part in this has only just begun. You're about to be led on a journey that you wouldn't believe if I tried to explain it to you. But you will believe it when you live it. Do you understand?"

"No, not really."

"You will," Marco said. "By the time this is finished you will certainly understand."

I thought I had left the whole thing behind me. Meeting Marco had been an amazing experience, and the roller coaster ride that came later was even more fascinating, but the fallout of screaming people and splitting heads was too much to bear. In the end I chose for it all to go away. I was living a full life and didn't need any more dramatics to brighten things up. There were more than enough things to accomplish, and this particular mystery had all but worn out its welcome.

But it wasn't going to be that easy, not by a long shot. Something was moving inside me, and it wasn't going to let me go until it finished its business, whatever that was. I could feel it growing and gaining strength, like a child in its mother's womb drinking the precious drops of life flowing between them. As long as I didn't push the experiments too hard I was able to keep the headaches at bay, but that only meant the Other was sleeping, not pushing against my temples with feet trying to break free.

The dreams continued but I was still not completely conscious of them. Something in my mind was resisting the message, holding it at arm's length in case it required too much too soon. The only thing that never changed was where I was and who I was with. The word "Bulgaria" saturated my mind even when I was awake, like an echo that wouldn't let me forget, pulling me and drawing me into its dark embrace. It wanted me, just as Marco wanted me, but they were holding their breath beneath the waves, and I still couldn't breathe in that faraway place.

But then one day, with the suddenness of a cannon blast, everything changed. To this day I don't know what made me shift the way I did, but the answer was so clear in my mind. I knew where I would find him, and I knew he would be there waiting.

One way or another I had to conclude this drama, and Bulgaria was the only place that could happen. The word pulsed inside my brain, and then suddenly it was out, breathing on its own, commanding its own life and way. If it had been anyone else, I never would have believed it, but the idea held me so close and with such an intimate embrace that there was no other answer. I was going, and I was going to find him.

I booked the ticket before I told anyone at the house. They would think I had really lost my mind, which was by then the common sentiment. No one saw it coming; in fact, they had thought my fascination with the whole affair had ended. The days of pulling everyone aside to watch my latest explosion of psychic power were over. I had practiced the Gift now and then without their being aware, but it was mainly just to see if it was still there. It was. If anything, my power had increased, though I had learned to control the unanticipated quakes that had so overwhelmed me before. Now, it was like a genie that slept in a cave somewhere deep in my mind, and it would only come out when I asked it to. When it did, I found that its power was unsurpassed, and this, if nothing else, is what told me it was time to leave.

It was the end of May, and I booked a flight to leave two days later. I made the announcement one night when everyone was home, and my concern about their reaction was unfounded. Everyone was in favor; as if they knew it was the only way for me to finally complete this odyssey. There were the normal, "Are you sure you'll be okay?" sort of questions, but other than that, it was unanimous. A day later I would leave for a country as mysterious as the night, and I would have nothing but my intuition to lead me on.

As I crossed the Atlantic, I could sense the approaching feeling of helplessness, as if I was leaving my home-court advantage and traveling to play on my opponent's turf. I remembered my last trip to Bulgaria and had never once felt a need to return. All the time I spent in that region of the world had been a turning point in my life, but I thought it was over. I knew that a large ship sometimes needs a mile or more to make a turn, but so much time had already passed and my life had changed so very much. I remembered when I came to Croatia in 1995, the year I first met the Emissaries of Light. How could I have known what would happen on that journey and how it would change my life? I wrote the book and began traveling all over the world lecturing and teaching what I learned from them. I did return two other times, and I swore that it was over. I had fulfilled some sort of karmic debt, and, as far as I was concerned, the bank was now closed. I had moved on to other things, and hoped my services would not be called upon again.

I had traveled to Bulgaria while the war in Kosovo raged. It was the only way to get to the area, since every other airport had been closed by order of NATO. I flew to Sofia and took a bus into Macedonia, then made my way to the refugee camps on the border. There was no real need to linger in Bulgaria, and so I didn't. I returned after the peace mission in Kosovo and left immediately, and that was it. There would likely never be a need to go back again.

So there I was, heading back for reasons I couldn't explain. I had no idea what I would do when I arrived, where I would go, or where I would stay. If there was any reality to the Gift I had received, then I figured it would lead me in the right direction. If not, then I still would have accomplished my goal. I would know that the whole thing had come to an uneventful end, and that would have been fine. No matter how I looked at it, this was the final act, and I was glad for it.

I arrived at the Sofia International airport on Friday morning. This is where the Gift would hopefully come in handy, trying to decide where to go and who to speak to. There were no signs that read, "Psychic Kids, 100 meters." It was also not the best opening question upon entering a country. "Thank you for granting me a 30-day visa, officer . . . and by the way, do you happen to know where they keep the psychic children in Bulgaria? You see, I'm looking for a little boy named Marco who taught me how to bend spoons and read minds. Any idea where I should begin?" I would have to ask someone, but I hoped I would know when to do it. For the first time since I had the idea of going there, I began to wonder if it was a good idea after all.

There were several small offices in the airport that acted as agents for local hotels and car rental companies. The first step would be to get a hotel, then branch out from there. I stepped into one of the offices to begin the search.

"Hello, I was hoping you could help me get a hotel in town."

"Yes, of course," the man said. He was middle aged and had dark eyes that were set back in his skull. At first I wanted to look away for it gave me a strange feeling, like looking into the empty sockets of a skeleton. He sat there staring at me as if he was waiting for something. I had no idea what it was.

"Do you need something from me first?" I asked him.

"Where are you from?" he asked dryly, a strange question to begin with, I thought.

"I'm from the U.S., from California. Why do you ask?"

"No reason. What kind of a hotel would you like?"

"I'm not sure, something mid-range, I guess. What are the choices?"

He sat looking at me again as if he was trying to decide something or was simply a slow study. "I recommend the Princess Hotel," he finally said to me. "It is very nice and I can get you a good rate. It is only a ten-minute walk from the center of the city and will only cost you $55. That includes everything. If you were to check in at the counter it would be $85, so I think it's a good deal."

"And it's a nice hotel?"

"Yes, it's very new and nice," he said. "Many American tourists stay in this hotel, and I assume that's what you are, a tourist, yes?"

I coughed. "Yes, I'm a tourist, here for a week to see the sights."

"What sights are you here to see?" he asked, testing me for some unknown reason.

"I don't know yet. I guess I'll have to get a tourist guide or something. Then I'll know what my choices are."

"There are many choices," he said, smiling for the first time. "Bulgaria is a very beautiful country. If you would like to rent a car to drive into the country, we can take care of that for you here."

"Thanks, but no thanks. I might change my mind, but for now I'm fine. I need to get my feet on the ground first."

"As you wish, sir."

I filled out the necessary paperwork and he processed my credit card. The whole time I sensed a deep uneasiness on his part, a suspicion I did not understand. As far as he knew I was just an ordinary visitor, straight off the flight. I hadn't even begun asking the questions that were sure to get me noticed. If this was the reaction to a hotel booking, I couldn't imagine what would happen when I really got down to business.

"Do you need a taxi to get to the city?" he asked me.

"Yes, I guess I do."

He opened a small window next to his desk and yelled into the main reception area where hundreds of people stood about waiting for loved ones to leave the customs area. "Jivco," he yelled, and a man came bolting toward us.

He looked at me and said, "You need a taxi?"

"Yes, I guess I'm on my way to the Princess Hotel. How much will that be?"

"To the Princess Hotel?" He paused. "That will be $15 U.S."

I knew I could probably get there for half as much if I pushed it, maybe even less. But getting ripped off as soon as you enter a country like Bulgaria is a normal part of the game. You need to simply decide how much you want to get robbed and then draw the line. It's going to happen; it's just a matter of the amount.

Jivco led me out the door and past all the "normal" cabs. The drivers looked at him with disdain, knowing he was stealing a possible fare. We walked past the parking lot to a row of cars parked along the curb. "Here we are," he said, as we came to a small Ford. He unlocked the door, and I threw my bags in the back seat; then we were off. As we left the airport he looked at me with curious eyes, sensing there was something different about me and the reason I was there. I was alone, certainly not a normal tourist, carrying only a backpack and shoulder bag. Just as the other man in the office had done, he couldn't help wonder who I was.

"Have you been to Bulgaria before?" he asked, as we pulled onto the main road leading into the city.

"Yes, once before about three years ago, but only for a couple of days."

"Why have you come now? Are you just visiting or on business?"

"Just visiting," I said to him. "I liked it the first time and wanted to come back."

It was a thin lie and he knew it. I should have been honest with him. *I'm a writer and am here to do research for a new book.* It would have been more believable than my original try. A writer I could pass for, but a tourist . . . I'm sure he had seen one or two of those and knew I didn't fit the bill.

"What are you here to see?" he asked. "Surely you have . . . "

"Actually I'm here to do some research . . . for a book."

"Ah, you are a writer." That seemed to help him. "Now I understand."

"Now you understand?"

"Yes, well, you look like a writer, if you don't mind . . . "

"No, I don't mind," I said. "I guess I'm not your normal tourist."

"You say you're writing a book . . . what kind? Maybe there is something I can help you with."

I had a strange feeling inside, like an opening or a gentle push, that said to pursue this further. As far as I knew Jivco was just a guy with a bad car hustling a ride or two, and nothing more. But maybe he would be the first domino in a whole series of dominoes that would all fall in succession, taking me to where I needed to go, straight to Marco. I had to trust that the Gift inside would lead me and inspire my direction. Why not begin right there?

"I'm writing a book about psychic children, and I heard that there are many of these in Bulgaria. In particular, I'm looking for a young boy named Marco who is said to be very powerful. Do you know anything about this or where I might find this boy?"

He look puzzled at first, as if he was trying to make sense of what I said. Then he smiled again and said, "Psychic children . . . that is very unusual. I can't say I've ever heard of this before." *He's lying, and I can feel it.* "This boy you mentioned, Marco, no, I don't know about him either." *That part is true, I can tell he doesn't know*

43

Marco, but he does know about the children. "Where in Bulgaria does he live?"

"I really don't know," I said. "I need to find someone who can lead me to him. If you know anyone . . . "

"That may be very difficult since no one talks about these things here." *Because they're afraid to, or not allowed to talk about it.* "Maybe you go to a church and find out."

"Why a church?"

"Maybe they will know more . . . I don't know."

"You said that people do not talk about these things here," I said to him. "Why is that? Are they afraid to mention things like psychic awareness?"

"Afraid is not a good word," he said in an anxious tone. "Maybe people do not want to talk about these things . . . maybe they'll get into trouble."

I had the feeling that he was trying to say something without really saying it. All I could gather was that he knew something, but couldn't talk about it openly. And I felt that he wanted to, felt it with my whole being. I just needed to find a way to make him feel safe.

"How does the government feel about this?" I asked. "Are they against psychic things?"

"I think that maybe the government does not like to talk about these things." *Now we're getting somewhere. I can feel him opening a bit.* "I don't know if they're afraid, but definitely cautious. We have had a bad history with this sort of business, and since the communist time, there has been reluctance to let it come back. The government is used to controlling the people and that's hard to do if they are doing psychic tricks."

"Why do you say tricks?" I asked. "Don't you believe . . . "

"Yes I do believe . . . I say trick only as a word because that is what some people think. But I knew a child once like the one you mentioned. It was a little girl and she . . . " *He's closing down again, like he feels he's said too much.* "None of that is important, and as you can see we've reached the hotel."

I hadn't noticed anything at all since we left the airport. I was too caught up in the conversation and the sudden mystery I found myself in as soon as I arrived. Jivco pulled the car beneath the canopy in front of the entrance and opened the door.

"All I can say is this," he said before he got out. "This is not good to go around talking about these things. You may find that it upsets people. I suggest you be very careful who you mention it to while you are here."

"Why are you so afraid?"

Then, he looked at me with eyes so dark that they shocked me. "It is you who should be afraid, not me."

I gave Jivco my name before he drove off, just in case he changed his mind and wanted to tell me more. And though he warned me to call off my search before it even began, I couldn't help thinking that I was already on my way. The Gift was buzzing inside my mind, a feeling similar to the one achieved by drinking five or six cups of coffee, and yet I felt so clear. I felt like a bloodhound catching the first scent of its prey, and then the sudden jolt of energy that catapults it forward. I had only been in Bulgaria for an hour, and I was already hot on Marco's trail, or so it seemed.

I checked into the hotel and then found my room. The man at the airport office was right; it was very nice and practically new. The elevator ran to the fourth floor, and I turned left down the hall. I was halfway to my room, watching the numbers rise as I went, when suddenly everything went dark. I dropped my bags on the ground and braced myself against the wall, then sank to my knees with my head leaning forward. I was going to faint, and there was nothing I could do about it. I knelt there for at least a minute waiting for it to pass, or to lose consciousness. Neither happened. Luckily no one came and I was able to relax into the feeling. That was all it took before I heard something, a buzzing noise at first that grew steadily into a low hum. I put both my hands on the ground to see if I could sense where the noise was coming from. The hallway seemed to spin before my eyes and the noise grew louder until everything stopped, and then it ended as abruptly as it began.

I knelt there for another minute wondering what had happened. There was something else that I couldn't quite describe, a feeling that I was not alone. I was being watched, but not by a physical being. There was definitely something there, the Gift told me that. But where and why? What did it want me to do or say, and why did it nearly cause me to pass out in the hall?

I stood up and walked slowly to my room, keeping my senses alert and ready. There was no one there at all, but I couldn't help but think that this was just the beginning of a long series of uncomfortable moments. Something didn't seem to want me there, didn't want me to find Marco, and I didn't know what it was. It hid in the shadows waiting for me, hoping to snatch whatever it could from my soul. I would have to be very careful and not take anything for granted. It was going to be a very long week.

I settled in my room and turned on the television, hoping to find something that would keep me awake until it was a decent hour for sleep. The way to trick jet lag is to forget the time zone you came from and adapt as quickly as possible to the new time. Don't even think about what time it is where you left, and no matter how tired you are, try to stay awake. Wait until eight or nine before even thinking about sleep. A little nap could mean a long sleepless night, so it's best to tough it out.

That thought kept spinning around my mind as I sat in the hotel room trying to stay awake. I hadn't slept at all on the flight, and now it was catching up to me in a big way. All I wanted to do was forget where I was and retreat into dreamland's sweet embrace. I would be safe there, no bending spoons or frightened taxi drivers, no psychic children and no Bulgaria.

The uneasy feeling I had in the hall was still there, but I was too tired to work it through. Was it just in my mind, the sort of odd sense one gets when they're in a country so unlike their own, or was there really something out there watching and waiting for me? If so, what could it be? I came there to find Marco so I could learn . . . I wasn't even sure what I was there to learn. For the first time since I had the idea to come to Bulgaria, I realized that I wasn't very clear on what I came to do. I knew that Marco held the key for what had happened to me in the last several months and what I was meant to do with it. But I had all but given up on practicing the psychic gifts he gave. I could feel the headache coming back, just thinking about it.

He brought me there . . . that was all I knew for sure. The dreams returned to my mind and I started to realize that I really had no choice in the matter. I had to come to Bulgaria for whatever reason, and I hoped the reason would find me. I was hopeful that I hadn't lost my mind, and there really was something out there guiding me, leading me toward whatever I needed to make sense of everything. The idea of heading home with my tail between my legs was too much to consider. Something had to happen, I was sure of it, and I had the sneaking suspicion that it had already begun.

I decided to leave the hotel and explore the neighborhood. It was six-thirty in the evening and the sky was beginning to grow hazy and gray. A light cover of clouds gave the air a heavy feeling that seemed somehow appropriate in this place. I walked out the hotel entrance and turned right down Maria Louiza Boulevard, which led to the heart of Sofia. There is a certain energy one feels in most former communist countries, a slow, slothful energy that doesn't seem to want to move. The buildings look like forgotten memories stuffed away in the closet where no one ever goes anymore. They are almost all the same color, a drab dirty brown with plaster peeling and falling onto the sidewalk below. There is no real sense of architecture, just an afterthought of lines and curves that fail to inspire. The same feeling seems to reflect in the eyes of most of the people walking down the street. I didn't see many pretty faces in Bulgaria, just the hard look of people who have had many difficult crosses to bear. Many of the women had bleached hair, which I thought could be an unconscious attempt to forget where they were. Most were thin beyond the point of health, and their smiles were a little too wide. There was more beneath the surface, the pain and suffering they had endured for years and would continue to endure. There was little else to do but smile and laugh and hope the deeper longings didn't leak out through their pores.

I crossed a small river that wound its way through the city and found myself in the center of Sofia. Cars passed blowing their horns, with teenage kids dressed up in the finest clothes, hanging out, screaming. They had apparently just graduated from high school and this was a local tradition. For a moment, I thought they didn't look any different from teenagers anywhere. It was the only time I felt an energy that resembled freedom and joy while I was there. At times five cars in a row would pass and everyone on the sidewalks would stop and look but not make a sound. I thought they were watching themselves, or who they used to be, and comparing it to who they were now. When the cars passed they cast their eyes to the ground to avoid the sinking feeling that rose inside them, the feeling that the best years of their lives were over now.

The cafes were filled and the smell of beer rose like incense through the air. The sound of laughter and car horns filled the streets, which were now surrendering to the long shadows of buildings and signs. It was becoming dark and the weekend was about to begin. A whole new light could now rise, not a physical light, but one that would help them forget the darkened forms they had wrestled with all week long. They could run without ever leaving their chairs, and hide from their own feelings of despair and hopelessness. Maybe it was my imagination, or maybe I was picking up the thoughts that flew around me. All I know was that the headache was back, and it was increasing as each moment passed.

I decided to head back to the hotel and get some rest. Eight hours of sleep was what I needed, that and an escape from the feeling that I had misread something by coming to Bulgaria. Who in their right mind would book a last-minute flight to a place with no plans and nowhere to go, trusting only their intuition to lead them to a child that might not even exist? I was so tired that I began to doubt everything that had happened to me over the last several months. Everything led to this journey, this ill-advised jaunt to a place where I didn't belong. Prostitutes lined the street as I walked back toward the hotel. They propositioned me in a language I didn't understand, but still I knew what they wanted.

But what did I want? Why was I really there, and what would I find? That first night was filled with far more questions than I had answers.

The next morning, I woke up at seven and was glad to feel the sun streaming in through the window. It was a nice room, and if nothing else happened, I could just stay there watching CNN until a week passed and it was time to go home. Then at least it would be over, and I wouldn't have to think about it anymore. But the headache! As I sat up in my bed I was surprised to find it was still there and had increased in intensity. It meant that I was getting close to something; that's what my intuition told me, but what that was I had no idea. As hard as it might be, I had to start asking people if they knew anything about Marco or the psychic children, in spite of Jivco's warning. They might be afraid to talk about these things, and maybe it was dangerous, but the sooner I got the information I needed, the sooner I would be able to leave. I didn't have to wait long for the next step.

I went down to the restaurant for breakfast, which was included in the bill. I was somewhat impressed by the selection, but I wasn't very hungry. I had a couple of eggs and coffee, then went back to my room to plan the day. When I opened the door, I saw a small piece of paper that had been folded and slipped underneath. I picked it up, then sat on the bed expecting it to be written in a language I wouldn't understand. It was in English, and it had my name written at the top of the page.

"Mr. Twyman, I know what you are looking for and might be of some assistance. If you want information on these children, meet me at Kiril & Metodi at noon today. I will tell you everything you want to know. Come alone."

The note wasn't signed. And how could anyone have known . . . unless it had something to do with Jivco. He was the only person I had talked to about the children. In fact, he was the only person I had talked to at all since I arrived in Sofia. There was also an energy about the note that I didn't like, and my head began to pulse even harder as I held it. Would I be safe if I kept this appointment, or was it some sort of a trap? No information came, just a feeling of deep caution. But in spite of that, I knew I would go, I had to go, for it might be the only lead I would get, and it had fallen right into my lap.

I went downstairs to the lobby to find out what Kiril & Metodi was. A young woman was standing behind the counter, and there were no other customers waiting.

"Hello," I said, then paused, the signal to shift into English mode. "I was wondering if you could help me with something?"

"Yes, sir, I will try."

"I have an appointment somewhere at noon but I don't know where or what it is . . . maybe a restaurant or a hotel." I showed her the slip of paper I wrote the name on. "This is the name, Kiril & Metodi. Do you know where this is?"

She stared at the slip for a moment and said, "Well, these are two Bulgarian saints, but I don't know if there is a restaurant by this name. One moment please."

She turned to a man who had just walked behind the counter and spoke to him in Bulgarian while he looked at the paper I gave her. They spoke for a moment then the man turned to me.

"I think this is a church," he said. "About two blocks from here there is a small church called Kiril & Metodi. I don't know of any other place in Sofia by this name, so it must be the place. Would you like a map that shows where you can find it?"

I said yes, and he took out a small map of downtown Sofia. Just as he said, the church was several blocks away on a street that was famous for its open-air market. It was perfect, I thought to myself. There would be hundreds of people there, and no one would notice us. But why would this person, whoever it was, choose a church to give me whatever information they had? I was sure this was the next step. My pounding head told me as much. I would have to wait two and a half hours for the meeting, but that would give me time to get myself ready for whatever.

I used the map to find the side streets that would lead me to the church. The problem with English maps in Bulgaria is that the letters do not correspond to the Cyrillic alphabet used in that part of the world. The road signs looked nothing like English, and yet I was looking at the English translation, which did me very little good. I was able to follow the map block by block, though, and before long, I could see the market in the distance. I also noticed the back of what seemed like a small church, but from the angle I was looking, I thought that it couldn't be the place. There was a tall chain-link fence around the building and the huge yard was overgrown and deserted. The whole neighborhood seemed an unlikely meeting area, unless, of course, this was the reason it was chosen. My head was pounding, and I considered turning back. I didn't have a good feeling about the situation, but what other choice did I have? To turn and leave would be the same as admitting defeat, and then I would never find Marco. Even if I was being led into a trap, which was bizarre and unlikely, I would have to risk it.

But why did the headache increase every time I seemed a step closer to finding him? It would fade for an hour or so, but as soon as my mind returned to thoughts of my real purpose, it would leap back into full view. It was worse when the Gift was working, when I walked past someone and suddenly "jumped inside them," as Marco had once described it. I would see dozens of what can only be described as television screens in my mind, almost like a vision that would overlap with my physical sight. Then, without any conscious effort, I would jump into one of them and see everything as if it was a movie. I would know about that person in ways that seemed impossible, and yet it was perfectly real, as if I was reliving the situation with them. It had happened three times as I walked through the street the night before, and so far that day, twice. I was learning how to make it stop once I was "inside," sort of like hitting the STOP button on a VCR, but I still had no way of making it not happen at all.

I walked around to the front of the church where the market seemed to begin. The street was closed to traffic and the center path was lined with hundreds of carts that seemed to go on for many blocks. Each cart was filled with fruits or vegetables, and as I walked further I came to an area dedicated to clothing merchants. It was rather well organized, like an open-air shopping center or mall, but on a scale much lower than what I was used to.

The street was filled with hard, rough-looking people, and it was difficult to push my way through the crowd. I could see the front of the church from where I stood and wanted to make my way there, but it was going to take several minutes the way things were going.

I finally pushed my way to the gate of the church, then slid by one of the stands set on the sidewalk. It was like leaving one world and entering another. Five or six people sat on benches outside the entrance, and the door was open wide, releasing the ancient smell of incense into the open air. The front of the church couldn't have been more different from the decay I saw in the rear. The building itself was well preserved and welcoming, and the yard was sufficiently cared for. I looked around wondering how I would recognize whomever I was there to meet. They would have to find me, not the other way around. No one sitting outside the church seemed interested at all. I stood there for a minute, then decided to go inside.

The Orthodox Church was very small, but there was such an amazing sense of history there. The dark icons were hanging everywhere on the walls, and old women walked about lighting candles and saying their prayers in front of them. The front altar was lined with at least eight icons, most notably those of Jesus and Mary in the very center. The drape separating the main area from the "Holy of the Holies," the most sacred place in this or any Orthodox church, was drawn. I looked around again and noticed two monks standing near the door, selling holy pictures and candles. They looked at me suspiciously, then looked away. I began to wonder if this was the right place, or if there was another Kiril & Metodi that I had yet to find.

"Mr. Twyman?" The voice came from behind me, in the direction of the entrance, and I turned around to see a middle-aged man wearing a black fedora and a tan suit. He was smiling at me and walked up with his hand outstretched. "Please excuse me for being late, but I had another appointment. My name is Alexander Minez, and I'm very pleased to meet you."

"Yes, thank you," I said. "Should we step outside where we can talk?"

He nodded and led me into the light, and I felt a lightning bolt shoot through my head, then the same dizziness I had experienced the previous day at the hotel. Then it was gone, and I looked at the man again. His face was hard and prematurely wrinkled, and he walked with a slight limp, leaning to the left from his torso up. I thought that this was strange at first, and wondered what sort of injury would cause such a disability. Then I looked back into his eyes, and they were unusually calm, the sort of calm I had felt before in monks. But there was something else that his eyes could not hide, something dark that lay beneath the surface like a shark waiting to rise and claim its prey. It was such a strange combination, I thought to myself, but there was no way for me to know which was more real, the calm or the storm. All I knew was that my head was pounding madly.

"I received your note," I said to him, "obviously, and am curious about why you asked me to come."

"Your curiosity is about to end," he said. "This is a very small city compared to New York or Chicago, and word travels very fast here. I heard a rumor that a young American is looking for some of the psychic children we have in Bulgaria, and I believe that person is you. Is that correct?"

"Yes, it is," I said, still trying to use the Gift to dive beneath the surface of this man and see what he intended. He was like a thick wall that I couldn't penetrate, only the calm exterior shown through. "I'm doing research for a book and would like to interview some of these children, in particular a ten-year-old boy named Marco. Do you have any information on these children that might help me?"

"I was hoping we might be able to find a way to help each other," he said. "I, too, am very interested in these children and have met many of them. I might be able to lead you in the right direction if you will agree to share anything that you might learn." *There it is, the first feeling of mistrust. He wants more from me than he's saying, far more than he can say.* "That way we may both get what we want."

"And what is it you want?" I asked him.

"These children are very special, but you already know that. There is much we can learn from them, and that is what I want, to learn." *Maybe to learn how they tick, so you can use them for your own benefit.* "You must feel the same way or you would not have come so far."

"Yes, I have come a very long distance, and I do want to learn from them," I said. "So, how is it you think you can help me?"

"Once you have found the children you're looking for, I can provide you with the opportunities to study them, all the necessary clearances."

"Study?"

"Yes, isn't that what you want to do? You are a writer and you want to do research on these children."

"And how can you get me this clearance?" I asked. "Do you work for the government?"

"Let's say that I have some influence," he said as he smiled and showed teeth that were near rotten. "I am connected with other people in Bulgaria who are interested in these children."

"And you can't get to them yourself, and you need me," I said to him. "Is that pretty much what it comes down to?"

"As I said before, I have had some experience with them, and yet I may need you to help me understand them better. That's why we need each other. You see, on your own, you will not have the ability to spend much time and learn what you came to learn. But with me . . . well, all that would change."

By then it was clear what was happening. However he found me, probably through Jivco, he felt I could be used to get him what he really wanted—access to the psychic children, and in particular, Marco. Did he know about him in particular? My pounding head was all I needed to tell me to stay away from this man at all costs, though I knew I couldn't let him know that I was on to him. Who knew how much power he really had?

"So if I agree to help you, then you can provide me with the clearance I need to study these children," I said. "Is that correct?"

"And a place to do it. These children are sometimes very hard to find, and you would be helping us all if you helped."

I suddenly knew why they were so hard to find, because this man was chasing them. Who knew where he was from and what his intentions were, once he found Marco. Was he trying to control or destroy them? It was very possible that the government was so frightened by what these special children were capable of that they wanted them out of the way all together. It wouldn't be the first time a government erased what it didn't understand. But it was more likely that they wanted to use the children to increase their wealth and power. Whichever it was, I certainly wasn't going to help, but I couldn't let this man know that. I felt like the Wisemen being asked by Herod to lead him to Jesus, and like them, I wasn't falling for it.

"I still don't know what will happen or if I'll have any luck at all, but give me a way to contact you in case I do."

"I have a very good feeling about this," he said, showing his sick, rotten teeth again. "I think you will surprise yourself, Mr. Twyman. And in the end, I believe we'll both get what we want."

I walked back to the hotel thinking about the conversation and plotting ways to avoid Alexander Minez in the future. Would it be that easy? I still had no way of knowing how deep his involvement ran or what he really wanted from me and Marco. The only thing I knew for sure was that he would never use me to find anyone. If there was any way to find Marco and learn what I came to learn without anyone finding out, then that was what I was going to do.

My head fumed as I walked and thought about Minez. He couldn't have played the villain better if he had tried, like someone who had watched too many Humphrey Bogart movies trying to imitate the "bad, bad anti-hero" who always lost in the final scene. Didn't he know how all those movies ended? Why didn't he send a beautiful woman to do the job, someone to shift the attention away from the ugly man in the black fedora and rotten teeth? Seduce me, but don't insult me.

I would have to leave the hotel immediately. Though I had no idea where I would go or where I would find Marco, I had to fade into the crowd and escape into the heart of Bulgaria unnoticed. Maybe I was being followed. It was unlikely that Minez believed he had convinced me with his ruse, but if he did, then I was home free. If he was naive enough to think that I had fallen for his rou-tine, then escaping would be a simple thing. But it was more likely that I was being followed that very moment as a precaution. I looked around and took in every car and person I saw, filing them away for future reference. It made me so angry, and I suddenly felt that my whole mission had been compromised.

Then I heard Marco in my mind, like the faraway voice from a dream sending messages to the living. The dream returned so suddenly, so unexpectedly: the conversation I had with Marco when he told me the real message of the Children of Oz. They had come to ask a simple question, he said, and to help people live the answer. The dream flooded into my mind, and I felt everything begin to change.

"How would you act if you realized that you are an Emissary of Love this moment? Begin!"

How would I act? How would I act that very moment? Isn't that what he was asking, how do we act when it's not easy being an Emissary of Love? It's one thing to be open and loving to someone who is loving us back, but when the opposite is true, when some-one is out to hurt or deceive us, what do we do then? Are we will-ing to see past the attack and perceive the truth in them? Are we willing to love that person in spite of their fear . . . in spite of our own fear? And what about Minez? If Marco's message is true then I would have to apply it to him as well. I looked around me again to see if I recognized anyone following me. What if I saw someone lingering behind trying to look inconspicuous, walking as if they were a shadow that was never far behind? Would I be able to act like an Emissary of Love, or would I run from them in fear?

There were so many people on the street, but none of them gave me that feeling I expected, the pounding temples that told me they were there for me. But I already knew what was happen-ing, that it was time to leave for the countryside where the real search would begin. I would have to trust my intuition, the Gift, to lead me to wherever Marco was.

When I arrived at the hotel I was surprised to see Jivco waiting for me in the lobby. "It seems you've been talking about me to someone," I said to him without stopping.

"What do you mean?" he asked. "I came because I have information for you."

"What I mean is that I just left a man named Alexander Minez, obviously not the kind of man I want to know, and he asked me to lead him to the psychic children. How could he have known anything about me if you hadn't said something?"

"I have been asking questions . . . yes, but I do not know who this person is." *He's telling me the truth.* "I decided that I could help lead you in the right direction, and so I did some checking around. Maybe someone I talked to . . . well, it does not matter now because I have something to tell you."

"I'm not sure who to believe now." Actually it was a lie, because I knew very well who not to trust, and was starting to believe that I could rely on Jivco.

"I cannot tell you anything specific," he said, "but if you want to hear what I do know it will cost you $50."

I looked at him and considered the possibility that I was being conned. If that were true, if he was making the whole thing up to make a few bucks, then he was failing miserably. He should be asking for more money and trying to convince me that he knew exactly where they were. Once I was out of the city, there would be no way to ever find him again, except at the airport, but that would be too late. He was just trying to make a little bit of money, and if he did have the information I needed, it was certainly worth $50.

"Alright," I said to him. "Tell me what you know."

"First of all, I was right about the government. They have a very big interest in these children because they think they are a valuable commodity. If they can develop their psychic abilities, then they can sell the children to other countries as spies. Can you imagine that . . . an army of powerful psychic children who can do anything from reading the enemy's mind to making them go mad. It could be the future of warfare . . . psychic wars. And the children are the key because no one has ever seen such powerful abilities before, even though we can't understand them."

"This is Bulgaria," I said to him, "not the U.S. or Russia. What makes you think that they would have an interest in something like that here?"

"It's a question of natural resources. There have been so many of these children discovered here, and other places around Bulgaria like Serbia and Romania. Maybe they are all over the world now, I don't know. But the government here thinks that they can control them and make money off them. That is what this is all about . . . money."

"So you believe that the government wants me to lead them to more of these psychic children so they can be kidnapped and forced into psychic labor camps. It sounds a little farfetched to me."

"Then why are you here?" he asked. "You obviously know what these children are capable of or you would not have come so far. You are looking for them for your reasons, and they are looking for them for theirs."

"If what you're saying is true, how do I find them before the government does?"

"I have heard that there is a monastery somewhere in the Pirin Mountains where they train some of the children. It is a big secret, and I was not able to find out which one . . . there are quite a few monasteries in that area. But I believe it is somewhere near Sandanasky. If you go to that city maybe you can find more. I believe that this information is true, and well worth $50."

He smiled as if he had just done me an enormous favor. And he had. My intuition said that he was telling me what he knew. The question was whether it was true or not. But it was the only lead I had, and one way or another I had to leave the hotel, and fast. If Minez was not having me followed, it was sure to happen soon. Maybe if I left right away I would be a step in front of them. That would be all I needed.

"Alright," I said as I took out my wallet and handed him a fifty-dollar bill. "Is there anything else you can tell me about this monastery?"

"No, that is all I heard. I heard that many children have gone there to be tested for psychic powers, and that sometimes they keep children there to train them. And I think I heard about the boy you are looking for, Marco. He is said to have learned there, and apparently has the strongest powers they have ever seen. He is very special, and so he is being kept very secret so the government won't find him."

"You heard that?"

"I am putting different bits of information I heard together and drawing a conclusion. I am not positive about anything, but it seems to make sense."

"You've more than earned your money," I said to him.

"Maybe I should have asked for more."

"Let that be a lesson to you. Find out how valuable the information is before you set your price."

I went to my room, packed, and checked out of the hotel.

CHAPTER THREE

THE PSYCHIC MONASTERY

There was no way to prepare myself for driving in Bulgaria. Once outside Sofia, I felt as if I had entered the Wild West, where traffic laws are ignored, and every moment is a frightening adventure. I wasn't even sure if the early-model Ford Escort I rented would survive the trip, let alone the other drivers whose erratic weavings were like suicidal daydreams. It didn't seem to matter what lines were in the middle of the road, or if there was a blind curve ahead with certain death speeding around the corner. Passing another car was a test of faith, and the oncoming horns were like old priests passing out penance in a confessional. I hoped I would survive the trip long enough to find Marco.

The map had once again proved to be useless. I would have to either learn to read Bulgarian or just resign myself to being lost. Finding an English-speaking helper outside the Sofia hotel system was almost impossible as well, and I found myself having to communicate with a series of hand gestures and a potpourri of words I learned from various languages.

"*Pardon, Grazie,* Sandanasky, *Molim,* this way?"

It was enough to communicate what I needed to know, and I was able to stay on track. The so-called highway was also becoming treacherous. The four-lane road had been replaced by a two-lane path almost as soon as we left Sofia, and the trucks and buses vying for position made for monstrous delays. Every half mile or so I had to dart into the oncoming traffic to avoid ditching the car in a pothole the size of a large television, and that meant always being aware that the oncoming traffic might do the same thing at any given moment. Sandanasky was 150 kilometers from Sofia, as far as I could tell, but the way I was going, that could take four hours.

As it turned out, it took longer than that. I didn't arrive until seven in the evening, nearly six hours after I left Sofia, and by then I was nearly exhausted. Sandanasky was nestled between several mountain ranges, which gave it the best climate in Bulgaria. Most of the journey was devoid of any real beauty, but I had the feeling that it was about to be redeemed. The hills and mountains rose in almost every direction, and the town had the feeling of a resort community. I had read in the tourist guide I bought that the area sported some of the best hot springs in Europe, and people came from many countries to enjoy its miraculous waters. It would be the perfect base for the next several days while I searched the countryside for a monastery teaching young psychics, as long as I was indeed in the right area. I had to trust more than Jivco for that. My intuition told me I was on the right track, and the buzzing in my head reassured me as well.

I checked into the Sandanasky Hotel in the center of the town since it was the only one that seemed reasonably nice. The hotel was attached to a spa, or so the guide said, and would be a good place to enjoy the hot springs. I parked the car and carried my two bags to the desk. The lobby was old and dark, much like my whole experience in Bulgaria. I couldn't help but notice a hint of suspicion cast in my direction whenever I said a word, and I wondered if it was me, or if they just weren't accustomed to seeing Americans. The women at the front counter were no different, and I had a difficult time getting them to understand what I wanted.

"I would like a single room for at least one day, maybe more if things go the way I hope," I said to the young blonde. I looked down at her identification badge, which had a snapshot of her, obviously taken before she bleached her hair, like half the other women I saw. It had once been long and brown but now it was short and blonde. Nothing wanted to stay the same.

"A single room?" she repeated. "I'm sorry, my English in not too good . . . is there anyone but you . . . are you alone?"

"Yes, just me . . . a single room will be fine."

"Just one bed?"

"Yes," I said, and I could feel my patience beginning to fail me after the long drive. "One bed or whatever you have . . . it doesn't matter."

"For how long do you need the room?" She said with eyes that meant she hadn't really understood a word I said. I had learned to recognize those eyes over the years. The mouth may be agreeing, but the eyes tell a different story. No matter how much they say they understand, in the end there is more confusion than agreement.

"I'll need it for tonight," I said very slowly, "maybe longer. I don't know yet."

"Tonight and maybe longer?"

"Yes, that's fine." I felt like we were finally communicating, and so I passed her my passport and took the key. She smiled and I smiled back. "Oh, I have another question," I said, wondering if it was a good idea to risk more talk. "I'm looking for a monastery that is somewhere nearby, I'm not sure how far away, and I was wondering if there is a guide or something that would tell me what's in the area."

"Oh, I don't know," she said, the confusion returning to her face. "There are many monasteries in the mountains, but most are very far away from here. I don't know where. There is one, Roshen Monastery, that is maybe a half hour away, but that is the only one I know."

I didn't feel anything when she said that name and decided it wasn't the right place. "Thank you then," I said, then walked toward the elevator. As the door was closing I noticed a man sitting in a chair in the lobby, and he closed the newspaper he was reading that very instant. It probably meant nothing at all, but my headache was suddenly running at full force. Was it possible that he was watching me, that he was sent by Minez to follow me to the children? It was more likely that I was being paranoid and was seeing dark fedoras around every corner. I had been very careful to watch for anyone following me when I left Sofia, and during the whole trip. As far as I knew there was no one on my tail, unless they were so skilled that they managed to avoid me altogether. Maybe the CIA could pull that off, but I had serious doubts about the Bulgarian government. As it turned out, I shouldn't have underestimated them.

I unpacked my bags, then left the building to explore the town. Beside the hotel there was a large park with a brook running straight into the village below. It was well kept with trees and benches occupied by dozens of people enjoying the last few minutes of the sun's light. It shone through the branches and cast long shadows on the ground, and I wondered if this would be the last night I would spend before finally finding him. I looked at some of the children that were there with their parents, playing in the grass beside the path while their parents talked and shared the details of their days. Could they be the Children of Oz, as gifted as were the ones I sought? Jivco said that many children had gone to this monastery to be tested for psychic abilities, and of all those tested only a few were kept there to study and learn how to advance their powers. There was no logical explanation for any of this, and it was too risky to ask too many questions. Word would get out and Minez would be on to me, if he wasn't already. I would have to trust the only thing that had gotten me that far, the Gift.

I came to a busy street lined with restaurants and bars, filled with people out for an evening stroll. The weather was perfect, and so I walked along, watching the people and enjoying what I could enjoy. The energy was much lighter than in Sofia, yet there was still no getting away from constant reminders of where I was, and where I wasn't. It was as if I had entered the Holy Land of Ritalin, a place devoid of the extreme highs and lows that might catapult one into either frenzy or despair. The cars all seemed to be similar, the houses, and the people, seemed to be on about the same economic and social level. I didn't see anyone who looked extremely poor, and no one seemed to be excessively rich. It was an impression that could certainly be challenged if I were to spend more time there, but I saw nothing to challenge my observation.

I felt that I had walked far enough in one direction, so I turned around to begin my journey back to the hotel. That was when I saw him again. He was nearly a block away, but when I changed directions I saw him slant his body to avoid my noticing him. It didn't work. It was the same man I saw sitting in the lobby when I was getting into the elevator, and I was suddenly convinced that my suspicions about being followed were true. I continued walking but kept him in the corner of my eye, never looking straight at the man. He had walked into one of the stores, a women's clothing store, and kept out of sight until I passed. Moments later, after I had crossed the street and was a good half a block ahead, I turned around with a jolt as if I had noticed something behind me. Instead I looked for him, the man who was assigned to my every move, and he was there, walking in my direction. There was no doubting it now. I was not alone in my search. They wanted to find the children as much as I did . . . maybe more.

I zigzagged down the street, always making sure he was still with me. If I couldn't lose him, I felt it would be better to keep him close, like the old proverb: "Keep your friends close, and your enemies closer." But was he really my enemy? There was a good chance he thought so, or maybe he was just doing his job, a third-rate intelligence agent assigned to keep his eye on a suspicious American. I wondered how much he even knew about the children. It was more likely that he had been assigned to watch and report my movements. And that meant that Minez was not far behind. He was sure to be there as soon as I found what I was looking for.

I turned the corner and waited there for the man to land in my lap. I assumed that if he was a professional, then he would swing wide on the other side of the street to avoid a possible confrontation. There was no way for him to know where I was, since he was blinded by the corner building, but it was a chance for me to get a good look at him, maybe even let him know I was on to the tail. But would that be enough to end the ruse? Probably not. For all I knew, there were three more just like this one, and if they weren't already there, they would be soon.

Seconds later, with his newspaper tucked beneath his arm, he bumped right into me. He didn't swing wide, and so there was no way for him to avoid my discovery. I actually grabbed hold of his arm as if I was startled by his sloppiness. But no matter how startled I seemed to be, it was nothing compared to the look of horror on his face.

"Excuse me," I said in English, moving him to the side while holding the grip a second longer than would be comfortable for him. Then, I walked away toward the hotel, and he had no choice but to watch me leave. There was no way he could continue his surveillance, and unless there were others watching with him, I was in the clear at least for the moment. I nearly ran down the street as if it would make a difference. It surely didn't, but when I walked into the hotel I couldn't have been more surprised.

"Hello, Mr. Twyman; it's nice to see you again."

It was Minez, the conductor of the whole symphony. He was sitting in a black armchair across from the front door, the perfect place to see whoever walked in or out. The spy game was over, and so he had no choice but to bring it out into the open.

"Why aren't I surprised?" I asked him. "Maybe you should send your friends back to summer camp to learn proper tailing protocol. They may as well be wearing signs."

He laughed and walked over to me. I tried to keep walking but he blocked my way to the elevator. "Yes, I know, they are not very good at their job, but then again this is not a normal thing for us. We are not used to being so persistent."

"And who is 'we?'" I asked. "You may as well tell me everything since I only believed your other story for about a minute."

"You're right. There's no need to hide anymore. I didn't think you would help me willingly, but there was at least a chance. Maybe you were not so bright . . . I'm sorry to see that you are."

"Thank you for the compliment, but I would rather hear the real story, then go to bed, if you don't mind."

"Please, come and have a seat and I will tell you what I can," he said, motioning for me to follow him over to the couches in the corner. "It is really more simple than you might imagine. I am going to tell you the truth, then make you a real offer. Obviously my last attempt failed, so we will both be more honest this time."

I sat in one of the chairs, and he fell into the couch. That is the only way to describe what it was like, since the cushion was so thick, but it seemed to have a deeper significance as well. He was slow and sloppy, and I could maybe use that to my advantage. I wasn't interested in anything he had to say as it was clear we had different goals in mind. But I had to make it seem as if I was playing along, at least until I was able to lose him for good.

"As I told you before," he began, "I am very interested in what these children are capable of . . . and there are many other people like me. The world is in the midst of a strange chaos today, and that means we must be creative in how we deal with our new problems. It used to be so simple when there were two superpowers, but now there is only one, and many more are vying for position. To find your way in such a world you need to use every advantage, and these children represent such an advantage. There are many people who would pay very good money to teach these children to use their powers for political advantage. Imagine the possibilities. It would be like entering into the mind of your enemy, or making them do what you want them to do. I believe it is possible, and I have in fact proven that it is. But we need more evidence, and that can only come with the help of these special children."

"So, what does this have to do with me?" I asked him.

"You seem to have a way to find where these children are being hidden," he continued, grinding his teeth as he paused between each sentence. "We know that there is a monastery somewhere near here, but even with our resources we have not been able to find it. Who knows why, maybe the children themselves are blocking us. But they aren't blocking you, and that is why you are so valuable. I believe you will find this monastery and then the children, and I would like you to then contact me. We will, of course, take very good care of them, so you have nothing to worry about. In fact, we will not do anything without their parents' consent, but when they hear why we need their children, they will surely agree.

If you do help us you will be paid very well . . . very well indeed. As I said to you, I am representing some very rich and powerful men."

"How do you know I want money?" I asked. "Maybe I'm in this for a whole different reason."

"We are all in it for the money," he laughed. "You may think you are here for other reasons, Mr. Twyman, but in the end it is power and money that we rely on. These children ultimately mean nothing to you. You will soon be on your flight back to America and will never see them again. Why not leave with a Swiss bank account stuffed with money? I can make that happen very quickly, but only if you help me."

"I have a feeling that finding you will not be hard," I said as I stood up to leave. "I'm bound to bump into one of your employees again. For now, I need to think about your offer."

"Think all you want," he said, as he stood up, then held out a skeletal hand. "You are right, I will be nearby. I'm confident in your American sensibilities. In the end you will see that this is the best way to benefit everyone. You will be rich, the children will be safe, and I will have what I want."

"By the way," I asked him as I began walking away. "Why do you think the children are blocking you from finding where they are, if it's in their best interests that you find them, I mean?"

"Because of what the monks at this monastery are saying, of course. They are afraid of us, and so they make sure the children are afraid of us as well. But there is no need, as you yourself will find out, Mr. Twyman."

"Yes, we'll see."

My alarm clock woke me up at 3:30 A.M., and I prepared to leave the hotel. There was a good chance that whoever was watching me was less than attentive, especially so early, and I hoped I could slide out the side door without being noticed. The staircase led to the lobby but on a different side from the elevator, which was more than likely where they would be. The sound of the elevator door opening would be enough to wake them, but quiet steps on the carpeted floor may not. I grabbed my backpack and closed the door behind me. The hallway was dark except for two small lamps at each end. I made my way to the staircase and walked the three flights to the first floor.

I looked around to see if there was anyone standing near the front counter. The office light was on, but no one was paying attention. It would be easy to round the corner and be out the door before anyone noticed me. There didn't seem to be anyone else there, but there would be about a two-second period when I would be exposed to the whole lobby. If there were someone waiting, and if they were paying attention, I would be seen, and that would mean my plan had failed. There was no need to resume my search for Marco if they were right behind me. And if I did make it outside, there was no guarantee that someone wouldn't be on duty there. It was a risk no matter how I looked at it, but there was no other way to continue my journey alone.

As I walked the three or four steps through the main part of the lobby before turning the corner to safety, I looked quickly to my left toward the elevators. There was a man sitting nearby, just as I expected there to be, and at first I thought he saw me. He was looking straight ahead in my direction and I stood still to see if he moved. He didn't. He was asleep, and as long as I was quiet I was safe. I wished I could be there when Minez heard the news that I had simply walked out the door beneath his nose. I wanted to see the look on his face, especially when he realized I had no intention of helping him.

Once outside, I looked around and didn't notice any activity. I walked to the car, started it, and drove into the dark streets of Sandanasky. There were no helicopters following me, no bugs on the bottom of my car, just one man who couldn't even keep his eyes open. I knew I had dodged a bullet, and I wondered if I had done it alone. The thought occurred to me that the children had helped in some way. Minez certainly believed they were powerful enough to block his finding the monastery, so why couldn't they have coaxed a man into a deep sleep? The possibility was there, but the reality was that I was free of them, at least for a while.

I took the road that left town, then turned on to the tiny highway that led west toward Greece. It would be a good place to start my search since the map I had showed three of four monasteries within fifty miles of each other there. The chance that the monastery I was looking for, the one that hides and trains psychic children, was actually on the map I had was slim. But I had to start somewhere, and it was the only logical move. Would logic even help me at this point? The only thing I believed was that if the children wanted me to find them I would, not because I followed a map, but because they drew me there. Then there was the Gift, the thing that had led me thus far. My heightened intuition was my strongest ally, and even Minez realized I had an advantage over him. It was the best chance I had, and yet I had decided to leave no stone unturned. I would begin by visiting the monasteries on the map.

As I drove, I thought about Minez and his thugs. He didn't work for any legitimate government agency or he would have had an easier time following me. There would have been more men or the warning would have been more severe. He was clearly an independent contractor, employed perhaps by other governments to deliver a particular natural resource for political exploitation. The natural resource in question was children, and that was something I could not stand. It was obvious from our last discussion that he was in it for the money, and he expected me to be the same. Lucky for me that his associates were not particularly good at their job, otherwise I would not be where I was. I kept looking behind me to see if there was anyone there. No one was following me, I was certain of it. The sun had yet to rise, but the light was just beginning to glow behind the mountains. A half hour later it would be morning, and I would be far away from the city.

By noon I had visited two monasteries I had found on the map, and neither of them felt right. It wasn't what I saw that told me that, but rather what I didn't feel. I was sure that I would know when I was there, just like I was sure a spoon was going to bend when it was in my hand. It's impossible to explain that kind of certainty, but I know when it is there. There was only one monastery left on the map I held, and I figured it would be the same story. Two hours later I arrived and got out of the car to investigate.

As I walked around the outside of the church I had the sense that I was nowhere near Marco and the others, but I also felt that there was something I could learn. There was a connection of some type between this monastery and the one I was looking for. Maybe it was the same order of priests, or maybe someone there knew something that would help me. I walked to the entrance and went inside. It was a typical Eastern Orthodox church with icons and candles burning in every corner. The smell of incense filled the ancient structure and I saw an old monk in one corner fixing a candle holder that had obviously been broken. I walked up to him and stood at his side.

"Excuse me, do you speak English?"

He did not respond but motioned for me to follow him. He led me out the side door and into a room adjacent to the church. There was a woman sitting behind a tiny desk and he said something to her in Bulgarian. She stood up and walked away and the monk motioned for me to sit down. He walked away, and I was alone in the room. Not more than a minute followed before another priest, about the same age as the first, entered.

"You were looking for someone who speaks English?" he said. "I speak a little, but not very well."

"Yes . . . I mean thank you," I said. "I am traveling through Bulgaria doing research for a book. I'm a writer, and I've been told that there is a monastery somewhere in this region that trains children, very special children. I have been searching but I cannot seem to . . . "

"I'm sorry, but I do not know anything about this," the priest said. *He's lying. He knows exactly what I'm looking for and likely could lead me to the exact place if he wanted to.* "Now if you'll excuse me."

"Please Father, I need your help," I said, as I stood up to follow him. "I mean no harm and feel as if I've been led here. I met a boy a few months ago, a very remarkable boy from Bulgaria named Marco, and I need to find him again. Strange things have been happening to me ever since he touched me, and I don't know what else to do. I promise you that I am meant to be here." It was a desperate move, but I couldn't come so close and walk away empty.

He knew something, I was sure of it, and I had to find out what it was.

"As I said, I do not know anything about psychic children or anything like that," the priest said again. "This is a monastery. We have been here for over four hundred years, and I am not going to risk that over such nonsense. Now please . . . "

"Father, I know that you know where they are . . . I can feel it." I looked deep into his eyes and pleaded with his soul. "It's one of the things Marco left behind in me, the ability to see inside people. As I said, I mean no harm, but I do need to find him."

He looked into my eyes and his gaze suddenly softened. Then he looked away and motioned for me to follow him. He led me down a hall and into a small office.

"Please sit down," he said, motioning toward a chair. He sat down behind the desk. "My name is Father Anselm, and I am the superior here. You need to understand that you are asking a question that I cannot answer. This is a very complicated issue, and I do believe that you are not here to harm anyone. But if word gets out . . . it would be very bad. Too many people know already."

"What do you mean?" I asked him.

"I will tell you this," he continued, " . . . several brothers in our order have assumed the very important and dangerous role of trying to locate these special children, then train them. There are several ways they search for children who have the Gift. Sometimes parents notice strange abilities in their children, and they seek help. We invariably hear about this and investigate. But that is only on rare occasions. The brothers normally need to find the children themselves. There are three members of our order who travel around Bulgaria looking for the children."

"What is it they are looking for?" I asked.

"Oh, anything that is unusual I guess, any sign that might indicate powerful psychic abilities. But once again, this is successful only on rare occasions. Then there is the most common way. We have a summer program at one of our churches where hundreds of children are brought to engage in activities they would not normally have the chance to enjoy. While there they are 'watched' by several brothers who are trained in what to look for. Now and then, a child does something or says something that catches their attention. When that happens, the child is then taken aside and given some very simple psychic tests. On the rare occasion that they pass the test, more are given to reveal the depths of their abilities. Now, you must understand that there is perhaps one in five hundred who passes all the tests, so it is very rare. When a child is finally discovered that meets all the criteria, we consult with his parents. The brothers tell them how important it is for the child to learn to use the Gift in compassion and love, and that they are experts at teaching them this. If we receive their permission, then the child is taken to the monastery and lives there for a while. How long he is there depends upon the child and his ability. Then he goes home to lead what we hope will be a normal life, though I personally don't think that is possible. These children are anything but normal, as I'm sure you know. They are very special and have a profound lesson to teach all of us. You mentioned a boy named Marco. Would you please describe him for me?"

"Yes. He was around ten years old, not very distinctive looking but did have a mole on his neck, on the right side. He had brown hair . . ."

"You can stop now," Father Anselm said. "I know who you are referring to, but what you say is impossible. It could not have been Marco."

"Then you know him?"

"I know a boy that fits your description named Marco, but I cannot tell you more. You will need to learn it on your own."

"How will I do that?"

"I am going to do something that I have never done before, but I feel I must. I am going to tell you how to get to our other monastery, the one where the children are trained. You will get your answers there."

I was overjoyed to be so close, and yet there was something missing, something he wasn't telling me about Marco, and it filled me with dread.

"Is Marco there?" I asked him.

"I said that I cannot say more about that. You will learn every-thing later. One more question. Are you sure you were not fol-lowed here?"

"Yes, I'm very sure. There were men at the hotel watching me, but I left so early and . . . "

"They are buffoons, all of them. They are dangerous, but stu-pid. They may not be far behind you, though. You should leave immediately for the monastery. You can get there by the time it is dark if you hurry. I will give you directions now."

Father Anselm drew a map and literally pushed me out the door. He had gone from suspicious to enthused in a half hour, but I believed he was right about the possible dangers. Minez and his men would search the obvious places first, and this would be on the short list. The monastery I was being sent to was not on any map, and it would be the end of the road for them. For me this was just a pause before I reached the real goal. Marco.

I followed the map as closely as I could, but given the condi-tions of the roads, which were sometimes reduced to dirt paths, it was not easy at all. I was grateful that Father Anselm had written the names of the highways and roads in Cyrillic, the alphabet used in Bulgaria, instead of English. That meant that I at least had a chance of finding the monastery, more chance than I had origi-nally thought. Otherwise, it would have been like another planet, so foreign and strange, anything could have happened. As it was, I gave myself even odds, but they were increasing with every turn.

I drove along the two-lane highway for about thirty miles, then cut off onto a narrow road. Five miles later, the pavement came to an end, and I had to cut between dangerous potholes and overgrown paths. There were times when I didn't think my rented Escort would make it, once when even I thought it was too wide to squeeze between rock cliffs on both sides of the road. But it did make it, and I passed a surprising number of tiny villages that time seemed to have forgotten. Three or four houses and one tiny store were often the only things that made me notice it, and curi-ous eyes looked out at me as I passed. I wondered how they were able to get supplies to this secluded region. How did they communicate with the outside world at all? But then I realized that that was probably the whole idea. They didn't want to be bothered, and so I kept on driving, not stopping at all to ask for directions I knew would never come.

I had come to the edge of the world, and prayed I wouldn't fall off. The dirt path suddenly came to an abrupt end at the mouth of a large cave. I came to a complete stop and looked at the strange scene in front of me. There were no signs, nothing to indicate where I was or what had happened. Then a strange thought occurred to me. The mouth of the cave was big enough for a small car, and though I could not see where it went, I did notice a slight turn to the right about twenty feet in. Maybe it was a handmade tunnel through the mountain, I thought to myself. It made more sense than the alternative, that I was at the end of the road. As far as I could tell, I had followed the directions the priest gave me perfectly. But he never mentioned this, an oversight I was sure he didn't make on purpose. There was nothing to do but keep moving. I put the car in gear and inched my way forward.

It began to get very dark after about fifteen feet. I turned on my headlights but all they did was illumine the back wall of the cave. Then the turn came, and I followed the wall to the right with the tentativeness of a boy moving his hands up a young girl's leg for the first time. I could feel the sweat forming on my forehead, and I realized that my hands were gripping the steering wheel far too tight. I let loose and took a deep breath, hoping to calm myself before I was overwhelmed by claustrophobia. If it continued much longer, I was sure I would lose my battle, but just as I was about to abandon faith altogether, I saw a light ahead of me.

The cave turned to the left a few feet later, and I saw the opening twenty feet away. I had probably only traveled one hundred feet or less, but it felt like something far more critical was happening. It was a kind of initiation, a test to see if I was willing to see the journey through to the end. That's why Father Anselm didn't say anything about it. As soon as I crossed the barrier, I felt as if I had entered a new world. The terrain looked more alive, and the sky seemed brighter. And though the spring flowers had long since faded in most of the countryside I had seen previously, here they were as fresh as anywhere on the planet, and they seemed to fill the green hills with life as I drove on up a steep grade. A mile later I came to another small village, so I stopped the car and got out to take a closer look.

A tiny restaurant was in front of me, and three men sat on the porch looking curiously in my direction. One of them took off a straw hat and scratched his head, then said something to his friend. I was sure it was about me. I walked over in their direction, brushing the dust off my shirt and pants.

"Do any of you speak English?" I asked. No one said a word. "I'm looking for a monastery . . . I think it's nearby . . . monastery."

One of them seemed to recognize the word and pointed in the direction of another hill on the opposite side of the village.

"Monastery?" I said again, pointing in the same direction. He nodded his head, and I was sure I was there. I could feel it in my heart, even in my bones. The Gift seemed to jump forward and snap to attention. The moment I had been waiting for had finally arrived. I got back into the car and drove up the hill.

A mile later the path widened and became a normal dirt road again. Then I heard the sound of laughter somewhere in front of me, children's laughter, and seconds later I saw something that I could hardly believe. First, I saw the ancient structure of the monastery, a two-story building that stretched an impressive distance, covering nearly the entire top of the hill. There was a field in front of the building, and in that field there were at least one hundred children running about and playing games. They seemed to be gathered together in distinct groups, some playing soccer, others playing tag, and another group lost in a game of limbo. There was a large coach bus parked on one side, and I wondered how it could have made it there at all. There must be another road, I thought to myself, one without caves and potholes half the size of my car. Father Anselm sent me the back way, the most difficult way imaginable. But all that faded as I turned off the car and began walking in the direction of the children. I had arrived, and nothing else mattered.

Several women walked amongst the children, keeping a close eye on everything that was happening, and an older man, who was obviously the coach driver, leaned against the bus smoking a cigarette. Then I saw three monks wearing monastic robes and hats watching the children and occasionally writing something in small notebooks they carried in their hands. The monks stood at different corners of the field, each one watching a different group. No one seemed to notice me, or at least they weren't paying attention. Everyone's attention was on the children as they played. It was the only thing that seemed to matter there.

I walked up to the nearest monk and said: "Excuse me, but do you happen to speak English? Father Anselm sent me here . . . " The monk was startled and turned toward me with frightened eyes. It was almost as if he was expecting to see someone else, someone he didn't want to see, someone that could cause him great harm. Then his eyes softened, and he shook his head, obviously in response to my question. Then, he tucked the notebook into his loose habit and yelled something at the monk who was closest to the monastery entrance. That man turned and ran through the door, a distance of about thirty yards from where he stood, and disappeared. The monk closest to me motioned for me to stay there and wait. There was no fear in his eyes, but the surprise had yet to vanish completely.

About a minute later, the young monk came out with an older man, another monk who wore a different color habit than the others, gray as opposed to brown. The older monk walked with his hands folded inside the large sleeves, while the other seemed too anxious to care. The two separated at the far end of the field as the young monk returned to his original position watching a group of children playing tag. He took his notepad back out and resumed his inspection. The older monk never stopped looking at me, and he walked straight through the children until we stood facing each other.

"You asked for someone who could speak English," he said in a serious tone that was not at all welcoming. "May I help you?"

"I hope you can," I said to him. "I am an American writer, and I was sent here by Father Anselm . . . or rather, it would be more true to say he drew the map that helped me find you. I have been looking for this monastery for a very long time. I think you can help me find someone."

He looked at me with suspicious eyes, and his dark short hair seemed to straighten a bit as he considered his thoughts. "You say that Father Anselm told you how to find us?" he said. "Do you know why he would do that?"

"Because he believed what I told him . . . the story that led me here," I said to him. "It's a very remarkable story, and I think you'll enjoy hearing it as well."

A long moment passed as he looked at me, and my heart began to race. Then he shuffled his feet a bit and took his hands out from beneath his habit, motioning for me to follow him.

"My name is Brother Matthias," he said as we walked toward the monastery. "I have lived here for many years, working very intimately with children like the ones you see here today. But I have the feeling that you know that already." He stopped, then turned around and looked at me. "I have the feeling that you know a great deal about what we do here."

I didn't say a word, just stood there looking into his deep, dark eyes. Then he turned around again and led me through the monastery doors.

We walked through the wide door that led into the community courtyard. To my left there was a long building made of stone with two floors. Several wooden staircases led to the second story and the hall was exposed to the outside, not closed in by a wall. There were many doors which I assumed led to small bedrooms, probably the cells of the various monks. The bottom floor had fewer doors and seemed to be for common living. On the right was the church, an ancient-looking building with deep inset windows and carved icon images. Overall it was a plain structure, not nearly as elaborate as it could have been. Brother Matthias led me into the church and into a small chapel near the back. He kissed his hand then placed it on an icon of the Madonna that hung on the wall.

"This is our most prized possession," he said to me without looking away from the painting. "This icon has been in our order for nearly five hundred years, and has been in this church since it was erected. She is our patron, our beloved mother. And so I ask that whatever we have to say to each other be given to her first. Let us kneel before her image and ask that she accept us in whatever way will best serve our Blessed Lord."

He knelt down on the floor and I did the same. He glanced back at me, and I seemed to know that it was appropriate for me to bow my head. He didn't say anything, I just knew it. We knelt there in silence for at least five minutes, and I did exactly as he said. I asked Maria to take us and lead us toward the Light. She had brought me so far, and I was now so close. I was sure that I would see Marco within a day, that is, if he wasn't there at the monastery already. But I somehow knew that he wasn't.

Brother Matthias stood up and motioned for me to follow him again. He led me to a room on the other side of the courtyard, obviously his office. He sat down behind a very small desk, and I sat on a wooden chair across from him.

"Are you the superior of this monastery?" I asked him

"No, I am not the superior. I am only a Brother, not a priest. But you could say that I am in charge. They are two different things of course."

"How are they different?" I asked him.

"We do not have a superior . . . not really. Father Anselm serves that role, but, as you know, he lives at another monastery. This place you have found is very special, and so it does not fall under the normal rules. We do a particular job, and I am the one who watches over every aspect of that."

"What is the job you do here?"

"We will talk about that in time," he said, shifting his weight backwards in his chair. "I would first like to hear why Father Anselm asked you to come visit us. It is very unusual, you know. I am quite surprised, so I'm sure he had a very good reason. Would you be so kind as to tell me what you think that reason is?"

"I can try," I said to him. "I am a writer from the U.S., and I heard . . . "

"Yes, you already said that," he interrupted. "But there is another reason . . . I can feel it. It has nothing to do with your writing, at least not yet. You are here looking for something, or someone. Which is it?"

He smiled in a way that made me feel comfortable, so I sat back and tried to tell him everything. I told him about how I met Marco, and then what began happening a few days later. I explained how I became obsessed with the Gift and how it nearly drove me insane. But most important of all, I told him about the dreams, and the fact that I felt Marco was leading me to Bulgaria to find him. It took me nearly twenty minutes to tell the whole story, and Brother Matthias listened with great interest and patience.

"Why do you think Marco would lead you to Bulgaria?" he asked me once I had finished.

"I'm not sure," I said to him. "I thought it was to learn how to use the Gift he opened in me. It has completely changed my life and I need to know how I'm meant to use it. Am I to use it to heal, to teach . . . "

"Or to learn?" he said, raising his eyebrow.

"What do you mean?"

"Maybe he gave you the Gift to help you learn something, something you would not have been able to learn otherwise. Maybe it has opened you in some fantastic way, and now you are ready."

"Ready."

"Yes, ready to serve. Isn't that why we are all here, to serve one another and God?"

"I believe that," I said. "How can it help me serve?"

"That is what we will need to find out. But first, I would like to witness one of these miracles. I hope you will not think I am being presumptuous, but if I am going to reveal some of our secrets, I need to know that you are ready for them. This could be a great story you have told, but once I have actually seen . . . well, then I will know what to do."

"How do you want me to demonstrate the Gift?" I asked him.

He looked around the room until his eyes fell on small knife sitting on his desk.

"It is not a knife," he said, "but a letter opener. It is not very thick, and I would like to see you bend it with your mind. This is actually a very low-level psychic ability, but it is impressive." He placed the opener in front of me. "If you can make it bend, then I will believe you."

I looked at the light piece of metal and knew it was going to be easy. I always know when I'm going to be able to bend something and when I won't. If I can't bend it with my hands, then it is unlikely that I will achieve that goal with my mind. Maybe it's a mental block and there is ultimately no correlation, but it is a belief I can't seem to shake. But this piece of metal was light and flimsy, and I knew that it wouldn't present much of a challenge.

I touched it lightly with my index finger and gently rubbed one spot. The pressure I put on the metal was minimal since I didn't want there to be any confusion about what had happened. I simply felt the bend in my solar plexus, and knew that it would happen. Seconds later I could feel it getting very hot, then the bend occurred, so fast that it startled even me. I looked up at Brother Matthias and he didn't seem surprised at all, as if he had seen this a hundred times.

"That was very impressive," he said. "But as you may have guessed, I am not at all surprised. Maybe by the time you leave us you will understand what I mean. The things you are capable of with this Gift, oh my, it will make these little tricks seem like child's play."

"So now that you've seen what I can do, will you tell me what this place is?"

He paused then said: "This monastery has a very particular function. We find and train psychic children. We really just facilitate them in discovering how far they are able to push their abilities, and that is all. I say this because we can learn much more from them than they can learn from us."

"And the children I saw outside, they are being watched in some way. Is that correct?"

"You could say that it is the first step. We look for certain traits, certain abilities. Now and then a child stands out for one reason or another . . . "

"Father Anselm told me about the whole process. He also said that Marco had been trained here. Were you the one who trained him?"

"It would be more accurate to say that he trained me . . . but yes, I am the one. Marco was no ordinary student. He was one of the first and most powerful, and he was also the most grounded. His heart was so open, and his compassion was so profound. I knew that he was meant to do great things, and so it was such an honor for me to help him. It is an honor for me to work with all the children, but Marco was special."

"As I said before, that is the reason I am here now. I need to find him. He's calling to me . . . I can feel it. But I had to come here first because you are the only one who can lead me to him."

"Yes and no," Brother Matthias said.

"What do you mean?"

"Yes, I can lead you to him, but I don't think it is wise, at least not yet. It is more complicated than you think. I can see that you have been approached by some of our friends on the outside, the ones who are not so interested in helping the children, but in using them."

"They've been following me, but I know that I lost them."

"You have lost them for now, but they are not far behind. You are a risk to the monastery and the children here, but I do feel there is a reason."

"Tell me what you think the reason is," I said to him.

"I can't tell you, but the other children can help you find it. I believe that you were led here, and maybe you were led by Marco. But now that you are here, you must stay, even if it is for a few days. There are a few children I want you to meet."

"You mean the Children of Oz you are currently training."

He seemed surprised that I knew the term. "Yes, the Children of Oz. There are four of them here now, and I want you to talk to them. They are very special, and each one of them expresses the Gift in a different way. They will help you discover the real reason you are here."

I looked out the window at the beautiful monastery, the trees that leaned forward and gave it shade, and I listened to the sound of the children playing in the field outside the walls. It would be easy to stay there, but there was another reason for being there.

I asked him: "And if I stay, will you then take me to Marco?"

"If you speak to the children I will tell you everything you want to know about Marco. Meeting the other children will help prepare you for seeing him again. And there is another reason. I think that the children want to meet you, as if you will help them in a way you cannot realize now. You need to understand, Mr. Twyman, that this is the first time this has happened, but, like Father Anselm, I believe you were called, and I believe it is in Divine order. Do you agree to these conditions, then?"

"Yes," I said to him. "I would be happy to talk to the children you are training. I would be overjoyed, obviously. And then you will lead me to Marco?"

"Then I will tell you everything."

"Then we have a deal."

CHAPTER FOUR

INTERVIEWS

Anna

There was a knock on my bedroom door at 7 A.M. , and I stood up from where I was sitting to answer. I hadn't been able to sleep well that previous night. Just knowing what I was about to do the next day was enough to keep me awake for an entire week. I had been searching for so long, even before I left for Bulgaria, and now it was all about to pay off. I would meet with the four children living at the monastery, then I would be taken to Marco. If everything went according to plans, I would be with him in two days. Then, if I was lucky, all my questions would be answered.

"Good morning," Brother Matthias said when I opened the door. "Are you ready to begin?"

"Yes, I am ready," I said to him. He stepped inside my room and sat down on the edge of the bed. I sat back down in the chair.

"There are a few things we must go over before you meet any of the children. First of all, as I explained before, none of the children speak English. We'll have to see if that is a problem, for as you discovered with Marco, it may not be a problem at all. I will be with you the entire time and I will translate everything. You are not allowed to bring any recording or writing devices. You'll have to remember everything they say."

"Why is that?" I asked him.

"Because it will be hard for you to be truly present to the children if you are trying to take notes. You must give these children all your attention, otherwise you may not get what you came for."

"What if I can't remember?"

"I don't think that will be a problem," he said. "You will remember what you need to remember. I will also ask that you do not ask the children to do any psychic demonstrations without my approval."

"Well, that's implied since I won't be able to speak to them except through you."

"That isn't necessarily true," he said to me. "You will find that these children communicate on many levels, not just through speech. You know this to be true from your own experiences. If they mention a particular skill, like telekinesis or mind reading, be careful how you react. Your eyes will communicate more than you realize, and your mind may ask them to do something that may not escape your mouth. I understand that you will not have full control over these things. I'm just asking you to be careful. If there is something you would like to see, ask me and I will decide if it is appropriate."

"Agreed."

"I am going to bring you to Anna in a few moments. You will spend two hours with her, then we'll see if we want to continue or not."

"Can you give me a little background on her before we meet?"

"Yes, that is my intention," he said, standing up and walking to the other side of the room, then beginning a slow pace back and forth. "Anna is a very sweet girl . . . 12 years old, and she has been with us here for almost six months. I anticipate that she will stay maybe six more months, then return to her family. She came to us from the tiny village of Drouzhda, which is by the sea. Her mother was the first to notice her psychic abilities when Anna was around nine. Letters would come in the mail, and Anna would know what was written inside just by holding the envelope. Her mother began testing this ability by writing words or symbols on pieces of paper, then sealing them in thick envelopes she couldn't possibly see through. Anna's ability to know what was written was astounding. Her accuracy was almost one hundred percent. She also had a favorite game she played, which was making flower buds bloom by focusing her mind on them. She had apparently been doing this for years without her mother's knowing about it. She was brought here for tests, and we realized how special she was. The decision was then made to keep her here until she developed her abilities further, and to keep her out of the sight of the government, which at that time was unaware of her talent."

"Do they know about her now?" I asked.

"Word travels very fast when we find a child with such an open heart. Maybe a neighbor hears about it or the child does something in front of other people. Before you know it she's the talk of the town, and the government is not far behind. That is why we need to act fast so we can stay a step ahead. If they get to the child first, which has happened many times, then we are lost."

"What happens if they get to the child before you do?"

"Oh, that is hard to say. Sometimes nothing. You see, these abilities are ruled by the heart, not the mind, so when the intention is to control or misuse the Gift, then it recedes. That is why our focus is on nurturing the children and teaching them about love, the love we learned from Jesus. It is like watering a beautiful flower. If no water is given, then the flower simply withers away, but when proper attention is given, then it blooms. There have been other times when we weren't that lucky, though. I think that they are beginning to learn from their mistakes, and may even start applying the same strategy we apply here. If that happens, then we will be in for some real problems."

"Why do they want these children so bad?" I asked. "Do they really think they can use them as a new kind of weapon?"

"Yes, of course they do, and they may be right . . . though we'll have to wait to find out. As I said before, the Gift is the result of a higher frequency, and it is a frequency we are all being called to achieve. The children are just the prototype, or the evolutionary jump. I personally do not believe that these gifts can be used to hurt or destroy, but I could be wrong. It depends on how it is done, I guess. The Gift can be very powerful, and there may be ways of utilizing that power without the compassion that directs its course. That is why we are so diligent here, teaching these children the laws of love so they will use their power for the benefit of humanity.

"If you're ready, I'll take you to see Anna now."

We left my room and walked to the other side of the monastery, the only section I had not been to. There were five or six rooms on the first floor, and the narrow wooden stairs led to what appeared to be a single, larger room on the second floor. A monk sat in a chair on the first floor, and when he saw us approaching, he stood up, walked to one of the rooms and knocked. Brother Matthias led me upstairs and opened the door, which led into a large room without much furniture. On one side there were a chalkboard and several chairs, and on the other were two couches. A single throw rug covered at least half the floor, and beneath it was the worn wood of the hundred-year-old structure. Brother Matthias moved two of the chairs over to the couches, then motioned for me to sit down. I chose one of the wooden chairs.

"What now?" I asked him.

"Anna will be up in a moment," he said without sitting down. "Then we can begin."

A minute passed, and nothing happened. Brother Matthias walked around the room as if he was having second thoughts about having me there at all. I felt those feelings, but for some reason my head didn't begin to pound as it normally did whenever I read another person's thoughts. I was very relaxed and overjoyed to have this opportunity. Brother Matthias, on the other hand, was having to fight his worries and concerns. He was clearly the guardian of these special children, and though everything seemed to indicate I was meant to be there, he was worried.

Then I looked toward the door and was surprised to see a small girl standing in the doorway. I didn't hear her approach or feel her presence. Brother Matthias seemed surprised as well and jumped a bit before walking over to her and saying something in Bulgarian. He took her by the hand and led her over to where I sat waiting. She sat down on one of the couches across from me, then looked into my eyes for the first time. I smiled and she smiled back, but there was some fear in her eyes, and I realized why. She didn't like to talk about the Gift, and she knew that was why I was there. There was a part of Anna that wished she was like other children, but she knew she wasn't. She wanted to be home with her family and friends, but instead she was far away at a monastery with monks who loved her, but weren't family. She looked at me and suddenly realized I was seeing into her. Then she looked toward Brother Mathias and said something.

"She wants to know how long you've had the Gift?" Brother Matthias said.

"Well, about five months now, ever since I met Marco. Does she know Marco?"

Brother Matthias asked her, then said to me, "She has never met Marco, but she says she knows who he is . . . they all know each other. That's part of the Gift."

"Yes, I've heard that before. They seem to be aware of every child in the world that has the Gift. Would you ask her the same question she asked me, how long has she known she had these abilities?"

"She has known she was different for only a couple of years, but she has always been able to work with her mind. She just didn't know what it meant. As far as she knew it was very natural, and this is what most of the children think. They don't realize that other children can't do what they do. That is what gets them into trouble sometimes. They do something fantastic like bending a spoon or something, and then they're branded. Sometimes, people understand and are not afraid, but most of the time, people are very afraid. Maybe they think it comes from the devil or some evil force. Then, they feel isolated and alone. That's why we want to find these children, to help them develop their skills but also to teach them the foundation of love. That is all that is really important."

I looked back at Anna and smiled, sending her the mental thought that she had nothing to be afraid of. She seemed to feel my message and sat back against the thick cushion.

I am going to try to communicate the discussion I had with Anna as accurately as I can, though it is clearly impossible for me to relate it word for word. As I sat down to write, however, I felt that the essence of the conversation was still very fresh inside me. The words may change, but it is the essence behind the words that is important. Though Anna was the first of four children I interviewed, I feel I learned the most from her. I will also eliminate Brother Matthias's translation and write as if I was speaking directly with the girl, though of course I wasn't.

"Anna, I want to thank you for taking the time to speak with me," I said to her. "Do you know why I'm here?"

"You're here because you have the Gift. Someone gave it to you, because most adults don't have it."

"Why is that?"

"I don't know . . . maybe because they don't believe anymore, or maybe because they've forgotten how to do it. But there are a lot of children who have the Gift. They're everywhere and I can feel all of them."

"What does it feel like?" I asked her.

"I can't describe it. It's just there, like something you've always known about."

"I was once told that the children are building a kind of web . . . a way of protecting it and helping everyone on the planet grow. Is that true, Anna?"

"I don't know," she said.

"You mean, you've never felt this way before?"

"I just wouldn't say it like that. You see, the children aren't really building anything. The web is already there."

"Already there," I repeated. "Where is it exactly?"

"It's everywhere . . . don't you know that? The web is love . . . that's what I've learned since I've been here. Love is everywhere, because it is the only thing that is real. But it needs to be strengthened by people, and that happens when they think about it. So that's what the children are here to do, to think about the web of love and make it strong."

"Another child told me that there is a question you are all asking the world. Do you know what that question is, Anna?"

"Of course I do, we all know what the question is."

"Can you tell me?" I asked.

"But you said you already know what it is."

She had me. Anna realized I was trying to test her and she wasn't falling for it. I felt that she wanted to be open and share what she knew, but she was also afraid. She had pulled her power back inside because she didn't want to show me what she could do. I realized that it would be best to go at her pace and not push her any faster than I needed to.

"Okay," I said to her, "Why don't I tell you what I think the question is, and you tell me if it's right. Is that fair?"

She nodded her head.

"Good. The question has to do with whether we're ready to feel the love or not. The children are asking the people of the world to act as if they already are Emissaries of Love . . . to live as if it's already true. I believe that the reason you're asking this question is because it's only when we act as if it's true that it's activated inside us. We have to believe it before we can see it. Is that close, Anna?"

"It's kind of close," she said.

"Well, how would you say it?"

"The question is whether you're ready to act as if you're loved by God. People think that God doesn't love them, and so they act as if that's true. That's why the world is the way it is right now. They say with their mouths that God is there and loves them like a mother or a father, but they don't believe it in their hearts. But what would happen if they *really* did believe it? Then, the love that's all around them would start to extend from them to touch other people, and then everyone would be healed. It's really very simple. So the question just has to do with whether people are willing to accept what is already true."

"To accept what is already true?"

"Yes, because that's how we feel it. The children are here to feel what is true, and to help others do that as well."

"What about the psychic powers?" I asked. "Why do some children have them and others don't?"

"Everyone has them, and they're also not important. Love is what is important, and strengthening the web. When you feel the love, then things just happen by themselves."

"You mean the Gift?"

"Yes, the Gift. How did you get it?" she asked as she leaned forward, suddenly very interested.

"I met a child, just like you, and he touched me," I said to her. "After that all sorts of strange things began to happen. I was able to see inside people and move things with my mind. Can you do those things?"

"Of course."

"Do you like to do them?"

"Sometimes, but it can scare people, and I don't want people to be afraid of me." She sat back again as she said this, as if she suddenly remembered that she had a disease that has no cure. "I know that the Gift is to help people, but sometimes I wish that I could just go home and not do any of this."

"Tell me what you know about Marco," I said to her.

"I know him, but I don't. I know that he has the Gift very big inside him, and that he used to live here. Brother Matthias told me that part. But I have never met him."

"Do you know where he is, Anna? I really want to see him again."

"No."

Brother Matthias looked at her as if to stop her from saying more. Why? I made a mental note of this but didn't say anything about it then. For the first time I had the feeling that he was holding out on me, as if he knew more about where Marco was than he was letting on.

"There's something else I want to tell you about the Gift," Anna said. "You have to want to use it, otherwise it isn't very good for you."

"What do you mean?"

"It can make you sick, like it's doing to you. There is a part of you that's still afraid of what it means, and so you try to run away from it. But you can't, and every time something happens it makes you hurt inside. If you use the Gift to do something, it makes your head pound like this." She put her hands to her head and squinted her eyes. For just a second the pain shot through my skull, then was gone. She opened her eyes again. "If you would just relax and let it happen, it wouldn't hurt so much. Then it would get stronger."

"It can get stronger than this?"

"Oh yes, much stronger," she said with a smile. "You still have no idea. Let me show you something." There was a vase with a bunch of flowers sitting on the windowsill. Most of the flowers were open except for a few tight buds. I could feel her sending energy to the flowers. In fact, for a second I thought I could actually see a stream of light coming from her, at first very broad, then getting narrower until it was like a laser beam focused on one of the buds. I watched the vase, as did Brother Matthias. He didn't seem at all surprised, as if he was about to witness something he had seen dozens of times before. Within seconds, I thought I saw the flowers begin to move, then I realized it wasn't the whole bunch, just the one bud that she was focused on. It began to open, at first so slow that it was almost impossible to tell. Then it began to speed up and, within a minute, it was like all the other flowers in the vase.

"That's what you need to do," she said to me. "You need to stop being so afraid and open up. Then more light can come into you. Then you will look so much more beautiful."

She said these things with such innocence, but I could also feel more wisdom coming from her than I thought possible. These children were more than an evolutionary leap for humanity, they were spiritual masters returning to the Earth. More and more this idea came into my mind, and more and more I started to believe it.

"Anna, if you could say anything to all the adults of the world, what would it be?"

She thought for a moment, and just for an instant I remembered she was still a little girl, though the most incredible little girl I had ever met. Her eyes rolled back into her head as if she wanted to give the best answer she could. Then she looked at me and said, "I would tell them to realize how strong they are, and that the more they love one another the more that strength comes out. People are afraid of their power because they think they will hurt one another. But the more they hold back the more they *do* hurt one another. It only seems like there are a lot of us here. There really aren't. There's really only one of us, like all the psychic children that know about one another. We know about one another because we're joined together, and some day all the adults of the world will realize the same thing."

Ivan

Later that same afternoon Brother Matthias came to my room.

"Are you ready to meet another of our children?" he asked me.

I set the book I was reading down on the bed. "Yes, of course I am."

He motioned for me to follow him and, just as he had earlier that morning, led me to the large room on the second floor. I sat down on the chair, and he said he would be back in a few moments. He returned with a young boy that looked like he was six or seven. Brother Matthias had his hand on one of his shoulders and said something to the boy in Bulgarian. The boy then walked over to me, smiled, and held out his hand.

"Pleased to meet you," I said to him, as I stretched my own toward his. The boy turned back to Brother Matthias and asked him something, then looked back at me. "What did he ask?" I said to the Brother.

"He asked if you are the one they have been waiting for." He closed the door and came toward me, then sat down in the chair across from me as the boy continued to look into my eyes.

"What does that mean?" I asked. "Have they been waiting for someone?"

"Yes, they have," he said to me. "They all knew that someone was coming here that would help them do their work. As far as I can tell, that means letting other people know about them and asking their question."

"Yes, I know about the question. They all know it as well?"

"Of course . . . everything seems to relate back to the question in one way or another. It's strange, but it's one of the ways we always recognize the Children of Oz . . . they all know the question, though they all express it in different ways. When we test the children, we always ask if they have a question they want to ask the adults of the world. Most look at us as if they don't understand, or they say something very naive or ordinary. But every once in a while they look us straight in the eye and say the right words. 'How would you act if Love were present right now?' . . . or something like that. Ivan here, well, that's what he said. I think those were his exact words."

Ivan was still looking at me, then Brother Matthias said something to him and he turned and sat down on the couch. His hands were folded in front of him, and his feet didn't quite touch the floor. He looked no different from any six-year-old in the world.

"Tell me about his history," I said. "How long ago did you discover he had the Gift?"

"About one year ago," he said. "It all happened very fast. His mother brought him here about three months ago because he was causing a great deal of confusion. His power is primarily kinetic. He can move objects with his mind or bend metal, even break things when he's angry. Since he's been here we've helped him control the aggressive aspects . . . really no different from ordinary childhood adjustments. His powers have also been getting stronger, so there's no real telling how far he will go."

Ivan turned to Brother Matthias and said something, then looked back at me.

"Ivan heard that you're able to bend things as well," Brother Matthias said. "He wants to ask you a few questions about that."

As before, I will try to relate the conversation I had with Ivan as close to the way it occurred as I can. In order to make it easier to read, I have taken the translation out and written it as if Ivan could speak English, which he could not.

"Do you have a question you would like to ask me?" I said to Ivan.

"Yes. Brother Matthias said that you can bend things with your mind. I can do that too, you know. I was wondering what it feels like inside you when you do that. When you make something bend or break, do you feel like something in you is bending as well?"

I had to stop and think about his question for a moment. "Well, I've never thought about it that way before," I said, "but I think you're right. The metal only bends after I feel myself bend, though it's very hard to describe the sensation. What does it feel like to you?"

"I feel it bending, then it does. I try to feel how happy I'll be when it happens, and then I feel that happiness getting bigger until something happens inside me. Then I look at the metal and it is bent. I don't really know how it happens, but it does. It's the same thing when I move things. If I just think about it moving, it doesn't, but if I feel it move, then that's when it happens. I feel it in my stomach, really. Is that where you feel it?"

"Yes, I also feel it in my stomach," I said to him. "It's a very powerful feeling. How did you know you could do these things, Ivan?"

"One day I was playing with my brother and he made me mad, so I made a rock hit him in the head, but I didn't throw it. I just flew it through the air. I don't do that now, though." He became very sad when he said these words.

"Why?" I asked.

"Because Brother Matthias said it isn't nice to use the Gift in that way. I'm only supposed to use it to help people, or to show love. If I use it when I'm angry it makes me feel sick."

"Sick, how?"

"In my head . . . it makes it pound very hard."

"Tell me more about that," I said. "I've felt that pounding myself."

"When I use the Gift in nice ways it makes me feel good inside," Ivan said with the sweetness of any child. "But when I hurt people with it, it is really like hurting me. Brother Matthias said that it's because everything we do returns . . . or something like that."

He looked over at the Brother and smiled. Brother Mathias smiled back. Ivan's innocence was infectious, and I felt myself relaxing just being around him. He didn't seem to have the same wisdom I felt in Anna, but he was surely in a whole different world than most children.

"How is it being around the other children?" I asked him.

"I like it because they understand me more than the others. But I miss my mother."

"What about your father?"

"My father died before I was born. It is only my mother and my brother, so I'll have to go home soon to take care of them. Maybe I can use the Gift to do that."

"Do you know how you'll do that?" I asked.

"No, but I've been thinking about it. Maybe I can make the money come out of the bank and into our house." He laughed loud and clapped his hands together, but then Brother Matthias said something to him that I didn't understand, and he became quiet again.

"Or maybe I'll think of something else," he said.

"Do you feel all the other children inside you," I asked, "all the children around the world who have the Gift?"

"Yes." And that was all he said.

"What does that feel like?"

"I don't know."

"Does it make you feel happy?" I asked, trying to coax him a bit, all the while wondering why he was unwilling to talk about it.

"I guess so . . . it makes me feel nice."

"Nice how?"

He looked over at Brother Matthias, hoping for help. Brother Matthias didn't move. "It makes me glad that there are lots of other children who can see what I see," he finally said to me.

"And what do you see?"

"I see lots of things. I see how people are living and how it could change if they all lived the question."

"You mean the question that the children want to ask the world?"

"Yes . . . do you know what the question is?" he asked me.

"I'll tell you what I think, and you can tell me if it's right." He nodded his head. "'How would you act if you knew that you are an Emissary of Love right now? Begin.' Is that right?"

"Yes, it's exactly right . . . did someone tell you or did you just know?"

"I met a boy just like you named Marco, and he told me. He was from Bulgaria too, and he learned at this monastery. I came here to find him again. Have you ever seen this boy before?"

"No, but I remember him," Ivan said.

"What do you mean?"

"Well, I've never met him, but I could feel him inside. But now I don't. I'm not sure why."

"Do you think he's gone somewhere?" I asked.

"I don't know . . . I just don't feel him."

"Ivan," Brother Matthias said. "Would you like to demonstrate something for James? maybe bend some metal for him?"

Ivan nodded his head, and Brother Matthias took a spoon from beneath his habit. I wondered if he always carried silverware there, always ready for a quick demonstration when the mood presented itself. He walked to the other side of the room and put the spoon beneath a large ceramic bowl. Then he came back to the couch and sat back down.

"We've been working with Ivan on non-localized metal bending," Brother Matthias said to me. "In other words, we want him to be able to bend the spoon without actually touching it. We started off with small twigs and had him try to break them when they were in another room. At first, it was very difficult, and Ivan couldn't do it. But, when he realized that the amount of space between himself and the object didn't matter, he was able to break the twig with relative ease. We've just recently started working with metal again, but so far the results have been wonderful." Then he turned to Ivan. "Are you ready to give it a try?"

"I already did it," Ivan said.

"You couldn't have done it that quickly," Brother Matthias said, but I knew he was telling the truth because I could feel him doing it. The look in his eyes never changed, but I could feel the energy coming from him and I could almost see it moving in the direction where the ceramic bowl was covering the spoon. And I also noticed something that I had never experienced before. I'm not sure if I imagined it or not, but I felt I could see through the bowl. It was almost as if I could see the spoon bending, as if I had x-ray vision. Brother Matthias walked over to the table and picked up the bowl.

"Well, I'll be," he said, holding up the spoon, which was not only bent but was twisted at least three times into a spiral, something I couldn't even have done with my hands. "I've never seen you do it so fast, Ivan. You are getting stronger every day."

"He helped me," Ivan said pointing his finger in my direction.

"How did he help you?" Brother Matthias asked.

"I used some of his energy as well, because I could see him looking at the spoon. He could see through the bowl, and that helped me bend it."

Brother Matthias looked at me and said, "Is that true?"

"I think it is," I said, "though I don't know how I did it, or even that I was doing anything at all. It just sort of happened."

"This is very fascinating," he said. "I have never seen this before, but I think that the fact that you and Ivan share similar aspects of the Gift means that you can work off each other. That may have very strong implications. If we can bring children together who share the same kind of power, then they work together. This is something I'll have to think about."

I could tell that Ivan was getting tired, as if the effort of bending the spoon had taken its toll. "Maybe that's enough for now," I said. "But meeting Ivan has meant a great deal to me." I reached out and touched his hand. "Maybe we'll be able to work together some other time, and do something better than bending a spoon."

He smiled widely and nodded his head. Brother Matthias took him by the hand and led him out the door.

Thomas

The next day, I would interview the other two children who were living at the monastery. I wondered why I hadn't seen any of them playing or even walking around the property since I arrived. There was no way for me to know where they were staying or where they had their own classes, if that's what they were called. It seemed that the veil of secrecy was drawn even there, and I wondered why. Were they kept together or separate? Did they learn as a group or were their lessons conducted privately? These were some of the questions that ran through my mind, and I wondered if I would ever find out the answers.

There was a knock on my door very early the next morning. When I answered it, one of the other brothers stood there and, without saying a word, motioned for me to follow. I quickly splashed some water on my face, and without so much as brushing my teeth left the room and followed him down the hall and down the stairs. It was only around 6:30 A.M., and I remembered hearing the monks chanting their morning office while I was still half asleep. The sound entered my dreams and I thought I was back at my own childhood church. As I followed the monk away from the building and down a narrow path, I began to remember the details of my dream.

I was an altar boy and mass was about to begin. I was standing on the altar looking around for the priest to start the mass, and then I realized that the whole church was filled. The congregation sat there looking at me as if I should know what to do. I looked in the sacristy and no one was there. I came back out to the altar and still there was no priest. Finally a man stood up and said: "Go ahead and begin without him." And so I did. In fact, I said the whole mass on my own, including the consecration of the Blessed Sacrament, all the while standing there wearing an altar boy's outfit. And yet it seemed so natural, as if I was supposed to be doing it. The people came to communion and took the host from my hand. Then I washed the chalice and opened the lectionary for the final prayer. That was when the knock on the door came and the monk appeared, and next thing I knew, I was marching through an open field with him.

"Where are we going?" I asked. He didn't seem to understand what I was asking and shrugged his shoulders. Minutes later, we came to a beautiful outdoor altar surrounded by tall rose bushes. I could see Brother Matthias standing there waiting for us, and there was someone with him. It was a young boy, probably the third child I was to interview. The boy looked to be about ten years old and closely resembled how I remembered Marco to look. He had short dark hair and deep eyes that seemed to look right through me as I approached. The monk led me to the altar, where we stopped in front of Brother Matthias.

"Good morning," he said, then nodded to the other brother, who turned and left. "You are probably wondering why I asked for you to be brought here instead of the room where the other interviews were done. But before I answer those questions, I want to introduce Thomas to you. He is another one of our children." He said something to Thomas and listened to the boy's answer. Then Brother Matthias laughed. "Thomas said that he feels like you look, like you both should have been left alone for more sleep."

"Yes, he is very perceptive," I said. "Tell Thomas that I am very happy to meet him."

Brother Matthias did that, then turned back to me. "This is a very special place because it is where the first mass was said on this property. There was once a chapel here but it was destroyed about a hundred years ago. It is a very sacred place for us and the other monks, and I thought it would be a good place to meet and talk to Thomas."

"Why?" I asked him.

"Because we have found that some of the children, Thomas in particular, seem to do better outside. I think it has something to do with nature, being away from artificial environments. Besides, I have kept you inside far too much and it is such a beautiful morning. I thought it would be a nice change."

"Does Thomas have a special ability like the other children?" I asked him.

"Yes, he does. Thomas is able to look through things, sometimes even walls. I'm not sure if that is exactly what he is doing, but it is the best explanation. He is able to see other places in his mind, or read things that are written on pieces of paper, then folded up and put in an envelope. If you would like, we can give him something now, and he can hold on to it for awhile. It sometimes takes a little while for him to see it. He will sometimes talk to us and seem to forget about the paper, then out of the blue he knows."

Brother Matthias gave me a piece of paper, a pen, and an envelope and told me to walk over to where neither one of them could see me. I was then to draw a simple picture on the paper, fold it up, and seal it in the envelope. He would normally have someone write a word, he said, but since I cannot write in Bulgarian, and Thomas cannot speak English, he felt this would be the better option. I did what he asked, drawing a picture of a house with a bright sun over the roof. The sun had wavy rays of light coming from it, and the house had only two windows, both on the second floor. I licked the envelope and sealed it tight.

"Now give it to Thomas," Brother Matthias said.

I held it out to the boy and he immediately placed it under his armpit.

"What is he doing?" I asked.

"That is just how he does it. He always places it there and believes it works better that way. Maybe it does, or maybe it's all in his mind. I don't know. But now we'll wait and see if he gets any strong impressions."

Thomas said something to Brother Matthias in Bulgarian, who then responded in what felt like a surprised tone. Thomas seemed to want him to ask me something, but Brother Matthias didn't seem to want to.

"Is there something wrong?" I asked.

"No, there is nothing wrong," Matthias said to me. "Thomas keeps saying that he wants you to celebrate mass on this altar, but I told him you are not a priest, but he is insisting . . . I don't know why."

"He wants me to celebrate mass?" I asked, but by then Thomas was saying something else, and Matthias listened.

"He said that the altar boy outfit was only a symbol," Matthias related to me. "I don't understand, but he said that it is about the child within you, the part of you that knows how to use the Gift." Matthias listened again. "He also says that you celebrating mass is about the communion you need to experience with the Gift within you. Only then will you be able to help them, help the children fulfill their mission."

"This is amazing," I said to him.

"As I said, I do not understand myself, so maybe you can tell me what you think it means."

I told Matthias about the dream I had, which was interrupted by the monk knocking on the door. Thomas had interpreted every detail.

"Will you ask him why the priest wasn't there?" I asked Matthias. "I somehow feel that this is an important element."

Matthias asked Thomas this question in Bulgarian, then listened to the answer. When Thomas spoke, his eyes darted back and forth as if he was looking inside his brain for the answer. He was also shifting his weight back and forth, something he didn't do normally, only when he was accessing whatever data he required.

"He says that it is time for you to let go of the church of your childhood," Matthias said. "It cannot serve you where you are now, except in new ways. He said that you are trying to hold on to the old patterns and use them to help you do new things. It won't work. Don't wait for anyone, just stand up and say what you need to say, and the people will be fed."

"How does he know this?" I asked.

"How do any of them know these things? That's why they are here, to learn how to use the Gift responsibly. If Thomas really has accessed your dream, then it's the first time. I have never seen him do this before, but it really doesn't surprise me. They are constantly developing new skills, partly because they are around each other. Their power seems to increase when they are around other children like themselves, like osmosis."

Once again, I will relate the rest of the conversation with Thomas as if we had had it without an interpreter. We sat down on a bench in front of the altar and the conversation began.

"Thomas, have you ever seen what a person dreamt before?" I asked him.

"Maybe once or twice, but I've never told them before."

"So, why did you tell me?"

"Because you asked me to. When you were walking toward us, I could feel you asking me about the dream, wondering what it meant. I saw what it was and decided to tell you."

"But I don't remember asking you anything," I said.

"It was the thought beneath your thought. You may not have known you were asking, but you were. I heard it like an echo, and I knew what it meant. I've been hearing echoes like that for a little while now. At first, all I heard was the main thought. But then I heard the next level, and sometimes even a third, the thought beneath the thought beneath the thought. No one is ever aware of those, but they are still there."

"Do you try to read thoughts, or does it happen by itself?" I asked him.

Thomas thought for a moment, then said: "I think it's both. Sometimes I hear something, and then I can't help but listen deeper. It's almost like I can't help it, and it probably isn't such a good thing. Brother Mathias says that we should always ask permission so that we don't intrude."

"Thomas, a few minutes ago, you said that I had to experience a communion with the Gift, if I'm to help the children complete their mission. First of all, will you tell me what you think the children's mission is?"

"I don't really know how to say it, but it has to do with asking our question. Everyone needs to hear the question, and that is why more and more children are coming who have the Gift. But maybe you need to tell people that we're here, then it will make it easier for them to understand. That's why Marco found you, to bring you here."

Once again, I saw that look in Matthias's eye that told Thomas not to talk about Marco. If I hadn't been so intrigued by the children and where they lived, I would have chosen to be suspicious, but I decided to wait until the right time to question him.

"I'm sorry," Matthias said, "but I only want the children to speak about their own experiences, not someone else's. I told you that I would answer all your questions about Marco, and I will. Please, continue the conversation."

"Thomas, why do you want me to help you ask your question?" I said.

"I don't know . . . I'm not the one who picked you . . . someone else did."

"Marco?"

"I don't know, but maybe."

I could see that I wasn't going to get much further if I continued to question him about Marco, so I changed the subject.

"Do you want me to write a book about the Children of Oz?" I asked. "If that's what you want, I could do it very easily. I think that people want to hear this message, and they will want to know about you as well."

"A book?" he said as his eyes widened. "You could write a book about us? That would be great. What would you say?"

"I would write about my experiences with you and the other children, and I would write about the question you are here to ask the world. I think that many people would be interested in a book like that."

He jumped off the bench and the envelope fell out from beneath his arm. He picked it up and handed it back to me.

"It's a house with a sun above it," he said in a matter-of-fact tone. Then he became excited again and said: "Would I be in the book . . . would you tell them about how I saw your dream?"

"Yes, if you would like me to."

"I do want you to . . . that would be fantastic."

"Thomas, how long did you know what was written on the paper?" I asked. He looked away, then at Brother Matthias as if what he said might get him in trouble.

"I knew before you handed it to me," he said. "I didn't want to tell you too fast. I can't always do it that well, but with you it was easy."

"Why is that?"

"Because you have the Gift like the other children."

"Are you able to read the other children's thoughts like you read mine?"

"It isn't really like that," he said. "When you and I talk with our mouths we don't make it seem like a big deal, and when the children talk to each other in our minds we don't think it's much either. It's easy for us . . . it's just what we do when we're together."

"How often are you with the other children?" I asked him.

"Do you mean physically?" he said.

"Yes."

"I don't know . . . quite a bit, I guess. Every day usually. But when we're not together physically, that doesn't mean we're not together. I can always feel them. I can feel all the children around the world who are like me."

"I've been told that before," I said to him. "What does that feel like?"

"What do you mean?"

"Does it feel strange to you to feel so many children in your mind?"

He laughed out loud. "No, it doesn't feel strange at all. You should be able to do it too if you have the Gift. Can't you feel their thoughts inside your head? Aren't you aware of everyone else?"

"No, I can't do that," I said.

"Well, you will be able to. Pretty soon everyone will be doing that. It's just where we're going. That's what's right around the corner."

Sonja

Later that afternoon, I was taken to the room again and waited for Brother Matthias to arrive. When he did, he sat across from me and looked deep into my eyes. "All the children we have here are special," he said. "But you may find Sonja, the final child you will meet, very unique indeed. She has been here for only a few months, and she may stay for a few more, but her psychic abilities are stronger than those of almost any child I have ever seen, except for Marco. They are actually very close. And the love that comes from this child . . . it is amazing. I have saved her interview for last because she is in many ways the completion of all the rest. She has the ability to perform many of the same feats as the other children, but she does it only rarely. Maybe it is because her heart seems to be focused on only one thing . . . Love. She is the most compassionate child I have ever met, and her heart is open wide. I think that you will enjoy meeting her."

Brother Matthias stood up and left the room. I could feel my heart beginning to pound, almost as if I was about to meet Jesus or another ascended master. Seconds later the door opened again, and a small girl, maybe only seven years old, walked in the room in front of the brother. Her wide smile was like the sun, and her brown hair fell down to her shoulders, barely touching the top of her back. As soon as she entered the room, our eyes locked together, and the link didn't seem to break for an eternity. She walked straight toward me and without hesitation wrapped her tiny arms around my neck and literally fell into my soul. I could feel her there, touching and loving the deepest part of my being, breathing life into my heart. When she let go and looked into my eyes again, I felt like a new person, as if her arms alone were enough to soothe the whole universe.

"This is Sonja," Brother Matthias said to me, and his voice was like a distant echo I could barely hear. "She wants you to know that she has been waiting for you, just like the other children. They knew someone was coming that would enliven their mission, help them ask their question all around the world. They believe that you are that person."

Sonja never looked away from me as Brother Matthias was speaking, but held me in her gaze with grace and power. There was no way I could look away, either; I was completely taken by her Light, which seemed to merge with my own. There was suddenly nowhere to go, nothing to do, and no words to speak. I was being filled somehow, though I could never fully describe what that meant.

She said something to Brother Matthias without looking away.

"She wants to know if you have ever seen her before," Matthias said to me.

"Seen her before? I'm not sure what you're asking."

He spoke to her in Bulgarian and she responded without ever looking away from me. I felt as if her eyes were powerful tractor beams that held my own in place. "She said that the two of you have been together before, maybe at another time, another life . . . I'm not too sure. But she seems to be."

I continued to hold the gaze, and she seemed to be looking deeper into my soul than she had before. I felt my thoughts begin to fade into a remarkable cloud of light. At first I was blinded by the light and saw nothing but the swirling whiteness of the cloud, but then an image began to appear, very faint at first, but it increased until I could see it very clearly. I was a small boy living in Indianapolis, running through the backyard of my family's home. I couldn't believe the details I perceived, for I thought I had forgotten this place. We had moved when I was four, and I had only seen glimpses of the house in old 8mm movies. My brother was on the other side of the yard, playing with a plastic bat and ball while I ran around the yard, as if I had just hit a home run and was circling the bases. The back door to the house opened, and my mother came out accompanied by an older woman with white hair. She was our babysitter, and I felt so much joy when I saw her there. I ran and threw my arms around her neck and screamed with delight.

"Oh Jimmy, yes, it's me, Auntie Marmie. We're going to have a wonderful afternoon together."

When my brother realized that my mother was leaving us with the babysitter, he began to cry and ran to her arms.

"You'll be fine," Mom said. "I'll only be gone for a couple of hours, and Auntie Marmie will take good care of you."

I hardly noticed any of this. I was too busy hugging my Auntie Marmie to worry about my brother, or when my mother would return. My heart was filled with such love, for I knew that Marmie loved me. It was always an adventure when she was there. She would sit me on her lap and tell me stories about Jesus and the saints, and then she would put my brother and me in the red wagon and take us for a walk around the block. It was one of the happiest times of my childhood, but I had no conscious memory of it until that moment looking into Sonja's eyes.

And then something very strange happened. Sonja's childlike eyes seemed to change and became old and wise. They were Marmie's eyes, and suddenly everything made perfect sense.

"You were Marmie," I said to the girl. "I do remember you . . . from when I was three years old . . . I loved you so much then." And my eyes began to fill with tears.

"Marmie," Sonja repeated, and I knew she was aware of the whole thing.

"Yes, now you understand what I mean," Brother Matthias said, and finally the gaze we held was broken.

"How did she do that?" I asked Brother Matthias.

"Would you like me to ask her?"

I nodded my head and he said something to her I did not understand.

"She said that love lasts forever," Brother Matthias said to me when she finished her answer. "When two hearts come together, the memory of that joining is indelibly etched upon the soul of the universe. You were a child not much older than she is now, and now you have come back to her to give her a similar gift. You have come to help her spread love to all beings everywhere."

"That is the real mission of the Children of Oz?" I asked.

"Yes, of course. It is the only mission there is, don't you agree? The children do it by asking their question, but we are all called to do the same thing in different ways. You travel around the world singing your peace prayers, and in doing so remind people of love. I am a priest, and so I perform my priestly duties, but all for the sake of love. It is always the same mission, but there are an infinite number of ways to carry it out."

I looked at Sonja again and her brilliant smile returned. She had been standing in front of me this whole time, though I was completely unaware of that fact. She finally sat down in the chair across from me and our conversation officially began.

"Sonja, will you tell me about the love you feel, or the mission of all the children who are like you."

She laughed as if I had asked a very strange question. "I can't talk to you about love," she said to me. "If I could, then it wouldn't be real, because love has nothing to do with words. Many people talk about love, but they don't understand it. They think that it is something they can find, or which can find them. But that still has nothing to do with 'real' love."

"What is 'real' love?" I asked her.

"You did it again," she screamed with delight. "Do you see how hard it is? No matter how hard we try not to do it, it is almost impossible. We want to understand things with our minds, and then we want that understanding to come out of our mouths. But the mind cannot understand love, because it has nothing to do with thinking."

"So how do we comprehend love?"

"Are you asking me because you don't know, or because you want to hear me say what you already understand?"

"That's a very good question," I said to her. "I think it's a little of both."

"Okay, then I'll tell you what I know. When your heart is really open, I mean REALLY open, then the mind lets go of trying to explain love, and the mouth sort of shuts on its own. I guess . . . you become love, and that's what makes all the difference. You can't experience what you are unless you have a mirror. So, if you become love, guess what the mirror is that lets you see yourself?"

"I don't know."

"Yes, you do . . . I can feel that you know." She smiled at me, and I could instantly feel what she meant.

"Everyone we meet," I said to her. "Every person we come into contact with, is the mirror that helps us see and feel love."

"Yes. You see, I told you that you knew. I remember when I was that old woman, I used to hold you in my arms and let you feel how much I loved you. I didn't need to say anything about it, because you already knew."

"Yes, I did. I can remember how happy I felt when you were there. I also remember missing you when we moved, because no one ever made me feel that way again."

"But now you can do it yourself, right?" she said to me, her young eyes looking up at me with infinite compassion. "Now that you know where love is, you can find it on your own. You don't need me to give it to you. Isn't that good news to hear? You're not a little boy anymore."

"And you're not a little girl, are you?" I laughed through my tears. Brother Matthias also seemed genuinely moved by this conversation and sat back in his chair.

"Yes, I am," and as quick as that she was a seven-year-old girl again. But in her eyes I could still see my beloved Marmie looking out upon me. She jumped off the chair and wrapped her arms around my neck again. "The more I love, the more I'm a little girl. And you can be a little boy again, if you want. We're all little children to God, that's what Brother Matthias says . . . right, Brother Matthias?"

"Yes, that's right," he said.

"So what are you going to do?" she asked me.

"What am I going to do?"

"Yes, when you go home . . . now that you've heard the question and know what it's all about, what are you going to do with it?"

I thought for a moment, not wanting to give a pat, easy answer. "I guess the first thing to do is to live it. Then maybe I'll write about it. Maybe that's the unique way I can help you ask the question."

"You'll write a book about us?" She asked as her eyes widened.

"Yes . . . that's what I do . . . as long as that's what you want me to do."

"It is . . . I do want you to write about it. I want the whole world to know the question, and to really answer it well."

"You mean to really act as if they are Emissaries of Love?"

"Yes, that's the only thing that's important . . . to live knowing the truth . . . that's what all the children are doing now. And that's why we all wanted you to come here."

"I'm so glad to see you again, Marmie . . . I mean Sonja," I said to her.

"I'm glad to see you, too. And remember, if I can be with you now, after all these years, it means that I will always be with you. The Children of Oz are with all of you as well. That's a promise I can make to you."

Brother Matthias stood up as if to signal that it was time to end the interview. He took Sonja by the hand and began leading her out of the room. Before they reached the door, Sonja turned back around.

"There's something else I want to tell you," she said to me. "When you go home, you're going to have the chance to live the question. Some things are going to happen to you, and you'll have to remember everything you learned here. If you do, then it will all make sense, no matter what happens."

Then she smiled and walked out of the room, and I sat down in the chair hard.

Marco

That evening, I sat in my room trying to absorb everything that I had experienced that day, ever since I arrived at the monastery. Was this why I was brought there, to learn about the children by being at their sides, and only then would I be ready to see Marco again? The four children I met seemed to have strengthened the foundation of the Gift in my heart, but I knew it would not be complete until I looked into that little boy's eyes again and asked him all the questions I wanted to ask. Why did he give me the Gift? How was he able to be with me in San Francisco without ever actually leaving Bulgaria? And what was next? That was the most important question of them all. Now that he had planted this seed in my soul and made me just like himself, what was I meant to do with it? Would it continue to grow until I was as powerful as the other children I met, or would it slowly subside, a temporary wake-up call to the Gift we all have sleeping within?

I resisted the urge I had to take notes to remind me of what I learned from the four children studying at the monastery. It would be like it had been when I was with the Emissaries of Light in Bosnia back in 1995, I was sure of it. I didn't have any way of taking notes then either, but when I sat down at the computer to write down everything I learned, it all came rushing into my mind like a flood. It was as if they were leaning over my shoulder, having the conversations with me all over again. Would it feel the same? Would the children always be with me, just as the Emissaries are with me still? I could only hope that it was true, for as I sat there in my room, I wasn't sure I wanted to leave at all.

There was a knock on the door, and when I opened it, Brother Matthias was standing there.

"May I come in for a moment?" he asked.

"Of course," I said as I stepped aside. "I'm actually glad you're here. I've been thinking about everything I have learned since I arrived, everything I have learned over the past few months since I met Marco, and it leads me to only one question."

"And what is that question?" he asked, as he sat down in the chair. I sat on the bed across from him.

"What does it all mean? It's all so fantastic, and these children are obviously the next step on the evolutionary ladder."

"But you want to know how it applies to the real world out there?" he said, pointing out the window. "It's a good question, and I hope I can give you a good answer. I have learned more from these children than they have learned from me . . . that's for sure.

The main thing I have received from them is the understanding that we are all in this together. They don't want to be separated from the rest of us just because their psychic powers are so much more powerful than ours. But they also can't ignore where they are and what they are capable of doing, just because it makes them different. They would prefer to pull us up to them rather than have us pull them down to us. Do you understand what I mean? Their role, this question and everything that goes with it, is their way of waking us up to our own potential. They want to be the examples for a whole new world, a world based upon the laws of compassion and love rather than competition and fear. That's why the powers are really secondary to them, not the primary gift. The real Gift is the peace that exudes from them, from every pore. If we can see what they are and believe that we can be the same, then anything is possible."

"But what about these people who are trying to find or stop them . . . even abuse them?" I asked. "What if we're not ready for them, and people try to destroy them? Maybe it's still too early."

"Yes, there are people out there that are still afraid, and they will do whatever they can to stop what has been created here. But I'll tell you what I believe: I think they will fail. In the end love always wins, and this is the moment for love's greatest victory . . . and it will come through these children, I assure you. There are simply too many people out there now who are ready for this awakening. All the religions are preparing for it because there is no way to ignore what is happening. And, at the very center of it all, there will be amazing children with remarkable abilities. They will be the ones who will show us what we are capable of, and they will also demonstrate how to realize the Gift within. Without that, it is nothing."

"But there is one thing I feel you've been avoiding since I arrived," I said to him, "and that is information on where I can find Marco. He is the main reason I'm here, and though I'm overwhelmed by the other children, I feel he is the only one who can answer all my questions."

"You're right," he said, standing up from the chair. "I have been avoiding you. It's not that I didn't want to bring you to him immediately, or to tell you what I know, but I felt it would be better to wait. It was important for you to witness what we are doing here, and to see what Marco himself had gone through. He is still here in so many ways, though he has not lived here for some time now."

"So, he is back with his parents?" I asked. "How far is it from here? My flight leaves in only two days, so there isn't much time left."

"There is plenty of time left, I assure you."

The way he said those words told me something was wrong. I felt the Gift activate and I tried to probe his mind to see what he knew, but it got me nowhere. He had already learned how to guard himself from such intrusions, and so I sat back and waited for him to tell me what I had feared all along.

"What I am about to tell you is very unusual and strange," Brother Matthias said, "and it is also very hard to say. As I told you, Marco was my star pupil. He had more natural ability than any child I have ever met, and, as you know, I have met many. And the way he was able to shift into that place of compassion was amazing. I have never seen anything like it before or since. He reminded me of what Jesus must have been like when he was a boy. Imagine that, what it would have been like to be with Christ, to teach him and have him teach you when he was so young. Marco's heart was so open, and that is why I was so shocked when I heard the news."

"The news?"

"Yes. The news that Marco had died. He had been sick for a while, maybe a month, but no one could determine what was wrong with him. It was as if he was giving himself in a way no one expected, like Jesus gave himself on the cross, maybe . . . and in the end, the result was the same. Maybe he decided he could do more without the physical vehicle, as if it slowed him down. All I know is that he is still very much with us. The children feel him all the time and talk about him as if he is still here learning at their side."

Somehow I knew he was going to say this to me, but the shock was profound nonetheless. I sank into the bed and my head dropped between my shoulders. Nothing made sense, and yet, it all did. I couldn't shake the feeling of total abandonment, or the sense that everything was exactly as it should be.

"When did it happen?" I asked him. "When did he die?"

"Somewhere around the beginning of February," he said, sitting down again. "And when did you say you met him?"

"We met the end of January, presumably right before he died."

"Astounding," he said beneath his breath. "It was as if he knew he was leaving and had to get you here to us. And the only way he could get you here to us was to give you the Gift. Then you would follow your intuition here and you would meet the other children. It all makes perfect sense."

"But why did he want me to come here?" I asked. "It doesn't make any sense to me at all."

"Think about it. The children feel it is time for their question to be heard all through the world. They say it is time for people to realize that the question itself is true, that we are all Emissaries of Love right now. And what better way is there to spread this question than through a book that you will write."

"A book?"

"Of course. As you told Sonja, it's what you do. It is not the first time this has happened to you, you know. It seems to be your particular role, to take this esoteric knowledge and these experiences and express them to millions of people. And what you have seen here is perhaps the most important of them all. The Children of Oz are all around us, and I predict that, within a few years, they will be very familiar to all of us. Your book will prepare people for their arrival. If they know the children are coming, then they won't be afraid of them."

"Why would we be afraid of them?" I asked.

"We are always afraid of the things we do not understand. Your job is to help people understand; then the question the children ask will be the most important thing, not the phenomena. That's why Marco gave you the Gift and brought you here. It is so clear to me now."

"Will the Gift stay the way it is now?" I asked. "What if it stops? How will people know I'm telling the truth?"

"They will feel the love, and that will be all they will need. It's the love that counts, not the tricks. I have a feeling that the door has been opened and won't be shut again, but if it is, then you'll still have an open heart, and that means so much."

"I need to say something else to you that I'm feeling . . . it's very strong."

"Yes, I know," Matthias said. "You need to leave here immediately. The children feel the same way, as if your continued presence will threaten our safety. I'm not sure how, but I have learned to trust their instincts, and now you feel it as well."

"Yes, but a part of me doesn't want to leave. I want to stay here and learn more."

"The world will present you with plenty of opportunities to learn about the Gift," he said. "But for now you must return to the U.S. as quickly as you can. We don't want to make it easy for them."

An hour later, I had returned to the hotel to pack my things and was in the car, ready to leave. I looked back, hoping to see the children, but they were not there. I hoped that they would come out to say goodbye, but they never did. As I pulled the car to the entrance of the monastery property, I could feel something inside me, deep inside, and I recognized the feeling to be Sonja.

"Don't forget what I told you," she seemed to be saying. "I'll always be there loving you. There is no escape from that."

I took an early flight the next day knowing Minez would find me if I didn't. It was as if the children had never existed at all. The jet left the Earth and I was on my way back home. I looked down at the ground and felt that familiar mixture of sadness and joy.

"Everything is about to change," I said to myself. "I just wish I knew how."

CHAPTER FIVE

TENSIN

The headaches were gone, and I was finally at peace. Meeting the children at the monastery in Bulgaria gave me the feeling I could overcome any obstacle, and I would now be able to use the Gift in the same way the others had used it—in love and compassion. I left to find the boy that had opened a window into my soul, and though I didn't find Marco, I had received so much more than I expected. Now, all that mattered was sharing their message with the world, the understanding that we are Emissaries of Love this and every moment, and that all we need to do is open our eyes to that truth. Then, reality simply fills in the empty spaces that seemed so vast a moment before. Then, love makes so much sense.

I returned to the U.S. a new man, or at least with a sense of courage that I didn't have before. If the children I met could live their lives so freely and with so much love, in spite of the challenges they faced, then I surely could as well. When Marco first touched me and awakened the power to see further than I had ever seen before, I didn't realize the true purpose of the Gift. It means very little without a mind and heart centered on peace. Otherwise, it is nothing more than a strange curiosity, one that stirs the minds of people, but not their souls. Without the deeper vision the Gift offers, the power is of little real value.

I couldn't believe how interested people were in the story I had to tell. There is something about the innocence of children that reminds us of our own, and when word began to leak out about my incredible adventure with Marco and the other psychic children, it became clear that I had stumbled across something very big. I wrote a brief article recounting my experiences and e-mailed it to a few hundred friends, and I was amazed when it began being passed around the world. I was soon receiving letters from hundreds of people wanting more information on Marco, the monastery, and the children I had encountered. This was an important story, and I wasn't going to be able to keep any of it quiet.

I'm not sure if what happened next had anything to do with the story that was circulating, or if it was just a coincidence. I thought I had come to the end of this particular adventure and was ready to finally start writing this book you are reading now. I thought the ending was perfect, everything I could have hoped for. How could I have known that everything was about to shift again in a way I never could have imagined? I had just left for a six-week tour, a month of which would be spent in the U.K. The phone call from Sharon came only two days after I left Joshua Tree.

"You're not going to believe what has been happening here since you left," she said to me over the phone, her excitement so strong that I felt my heart start beating faster. I was in Chicago with my daughter, getting ready to leave for London the next day, and I wondered if my plans would suddenly change. "Yesterday there was a knock on the door, and when I went to answer it, there was a fifteen-year-old boy standing there wearing the robes of a Buddhist monk. There were two other people with him, apparently his guardians . . . I'm not really sure. The boy's name is Lama Tensin, and you're not going to believe the story he told me."

"You'd be surprised what I would believe," I said to her.

"Yes, of course you would." She laughed when she remembered who she was talking to. "Anyway, he was born in Greece, and when he was only a year old the Dalai Lama himself came to his mother and told her that her son was a great Tulku. Now I didn't know what a Tulku even was, but now I do. It's a Tibetan belief that great souls return to the earth after they die, lifetime after lifetime, to help other beings attain enlightenment. In this case, His

Holiness believed that Lama Tensin was the reincarnation of his former tutor. Are you following me so far?"

"Yes, of course I am," I said. "Keep going."

"Well, the boy was taken to India when he was three to study directly under the Dalai Lama, and remained there until he was seven. He then was sent to New York, where he was put into a university. Do you believe that? He was only seven years old and he was in college. He apparently has already earned two masters degrees, one in physics and the other in psychology."

"That sounds impossible," I said to her in disbelief.

"And he can speak seven languages. I'm telling you, Jimmy, this boy is amazing. But here's the best part. He said that the Dalai Lama himself asked him to go to the California desert and work with you. He's apparently been following your work for a long time, and now the stuff about the psychic children . . . as you know, it's really getting out there in a big way. It sounds like Lama Tensin is meant to help you with it."

I sat down in the chair to assimilate everything I was hearing. "So, this boy, this Lama, is staying at our house?" I asked.

"Yes, actually . . . he's sleeping in your room," she said hesitantly. "I hope you don't mind but Tensin thought it was important."

"Important? Why? I mean, I'm honored . . . really, but I'm not going to be back for about six weeks."

"Yes, I told him that too, but he said he'll wait. As far as I can tell he's not going anywhere until you get home. Everyone else at the house loves him and we have no problem with him staying here. In fact, there is an amazing energy present since he arrived. We can all feel it. I don't know what it means, but it fits in very well with everything you have been experiencing lately."

"It does," I said to her, "but I need to know more about him. Where was he before he came to the house?"

"He was with the Dalai Lama during his talk in San Jose, then came here with some people he met there. That must have been when His Holiness told him to come here."

"And what about before that? Do we have any idea where he has been staying?"

"He said that he was living with the Dalai Lama's brother in Indiana. I thought that was funny, but why shouldn't he be living there?"

"Has anyone contacted him?"

"No. But it might be a good idea."

"Yes, it probably would be," I said to her. "Not that I don't love the idea of it . . . it's fantastic. But if he wants to live at the house, we're going to have to be responsible for him. He is a minor."

"Lama Tensin was a little vague about the details of where he has been, but I haven't felt anything strange about him. To the contrary. He is so sweet and wise. It's really hard to believe that he is only fifteen."

"I know what you mean. That was my experience with all the children I met in Bulgaria. They are ageless in a very real way. Did you tell him about my recent adventures?"

"No, I haven't," Sharon said. "It's all happening so fast, I haven't had a chance to catch my breath."

"Now I wish I wasn't going on tour, but it sounds like he's willing to wait."

"That's what he says. Wait . . . he just came into the room. Do you want to say hello to him?"

I could feel my heart begin to beat faster, as if there was more happening than I was consciously aware of. "Yes . . . go ahead and put him on," I said.

There was a pause and I could hear Sharon saying something to him. Then he picked up the phone and said, "Hello, Jimmy?"

"Hello, Lama Tensin, it's so good to meet you. Sharon couldn't say enough."

"Yes, it is very auspicious to be here, especially after everything His Holiness said to me about you and the work you are doing."

"I have to say that I am amazed by that," I said to him. "How does the Dalai Lama know about our projects?"

"Oh, he was very impressed by the Cloth of Many Colors project you started, and he was in Washington, D.C., when you wrapped it at the base of the Capitol with members of Congress. He wanted to be there but was not able to come. That is why he asked me to come here now. It is so hard for him to go where he wants to go because of security issues, so he sometimes sends Lamas out to visit for him. His Holiness can look through my eyes and see what I see. I guess that really means that he is here at your house as well. It is a very wonderful feeling when he does that."

"Wow," I said, not able to find other more appropriate words. "And Sharon said you are willing to wait until I return."

"Yes. I will do whatever the Dalai Lama asks me to do, and this is where he wants me to stay for now."

"But what will you do while you're there?" I asked him.

"Maybe I will teach. I have been given permission from His Holiness to conduct some very high level initiations, so maybe that is what I will do. He will soon tell me what he has in mind."

"The Dalai Lama?"

"Yes, of course. I will stay here as long as he wants me to stay. When the work is done, then I will leave."

"You know," I said to him, "I have a daughter the same age as you, but she is very normal . . . well, I hope you know what I mean. She isn't like you. You seem so sure about what you're doing, so clear."

"I was raised to be a Tulku from the time I was one year old," he said. "I have always known who I am, and I can remember all my past lives. I've come back to Earth again and again to do this work, and I'm so fortunate to be able to have known His Holiness in all his incarnations. I was his teacher and now he is mine. The roles will switch over and over until there is no need for us to return at all. Then we will let go of the wheel. Then we will melt back into the ocean."

"Lama Tensin, I'm so glad to know you are there right now, and I will return as soon as I can."

"You never really left at all," he said. "I can feel you everywhere. I can see your face everywhere I turn. Do what you need to do and know that I am waiting for you."

It didn't take long for people throughout Southern California to find out about the amazing boy Lama that had landed in Joshua

Tree. As I toured through the U.K., I heard about the hundreds of people who were traveling from as far away as San Francisco to hear him teach, and I realized that we had a phenomenon on our hands. Joanne and her sister Nancy acted as Lama Tensin's coordinators and stand-in mothers. We were lucky that no one knew where our house was located, or there would have been no rest at all. People brought gifts and came with requests for him to speak to this or that group, or to come to bless their homes, or help them with their personal problems. I could tell everyone back home was exhausted, and that was only after a week. Who knew what it would be like by the time I arrived? By then the house could have easily been turned into a thriving Buddhist monastery.

Even in England, on the other side of the Atlantic, people had heard the news. It had spread like wildfire, all about the boy the Dalai Lama had entrusted with the holy task of initiating people into the high mysteries of the Buddhist path. I even met a young couple who were planning to fly to California just to meet Lama Tensin. As far as I could tell, the whole thing was moving quickly to the point of hysteria, but there was nothing I could do about it so far away. Joanne and Nancy were devising creative strategies for getting Lama Tensin in and out of the learning center, where the talks were being held, without him being mobbed by the huge crowds. The first talk he gave had maybe fifty people present, but attendance was doubling every time, as word spread. They all wanted a piece of him, and there was still a part of Tensin that wasn't able to deal with so much adoration. After all, he was only fifteen, and no matter how enlightened he was, it was going to be tricky adjusting to his new fame.

I had already met other children like Tensin, and so I had more understanding of what was happening than most people. I remembered what the Children of Oz told me, all about the need to look past the psychic phenomenon in order to experience what is really happening. Getting stuck on the outer appearance was not going to help anyone, and I felt that this might be happening at my home. It's easy to fall in love with a boy who was personally sent by the Dalai Lama because the story is so unique, so fantastic. But if it means separating Tensin's holiness from everyone else's, making him seem like a great saint surrounded by the unenlightened masses, then the real gift would be ignored. From everything I heard Tensin was trying to get people to perceive their own holiness, just as any spiritual master would, but the frenzy that swirled around him made me think that most people weren't getting the message. Big surprise.

I talked to Lama Tensin often when I was away, and I never lost the original feeling I had about him. He was authentic, I was sure of it. Even from that great distance, I could feel what he was doing, and I had no reason to doubt his claims. The background check I asked Sharon to conduct was set aside after only a few days, such was the confidence he inspired. There was no way for me to control what was happening, and I didn't feel any need to try. He was a gift from God, and I wasn't about to be disrespectful. After everything that had happened since the beginning of the year, ever since I first met Marco, I was willing to accept anything. Nothing was too strange or bizarre.

I remembered the last thing I was told by Sonja, the young girl I interviewed when I was still at the monastery in Bulgaria. She said that someone was coming that would teach me a very important lesson about being an Emissary of Love. Her psychic gift had obviously shown her the eventual appearance of Tensin, for that was exactly what he seemed to be teaching everyone. But there was something else in her voice that made me feel uneasy and strange. It wasn't so much what she said, but something that lay beneath her words. My own intuition told me to be very careful and pay close attention to everything that happened, everyone I met. But there was no sign that Lama Tensin was not everything he said he was. If anything, he was more than he said he was, and the proof existed in the transformation of everyone who listened to him teach. I was hearing miraculous stories coming from Joshua Tree, and I couldn't wait to return.

"How would you say things are going?" I asked Tensin the next time we spoke on the phone.

"It is very sweet, except for the people who want to suck me dry," he said.

I suddenly felt my antenna go up, that part of me that watches a person's every movement, then compares the received information with a long list of other stimuli that might help me decide if I should be concerned about what I am hearing. I could feel the Gift leap forward, perhaps for the first time since I heard about Tensin. "What do you mean?" I asked him.

"There are people here who want to take my energy for themselves because they don't think they have enough themselves. After I teach, I feel exhausted and need to rest for a day or two. I'm afraid I'm under some kind of psychic attack, and I can feel His Holiness being very concerned."

"I think you're right about some people relying upon you to show them who they are," I said, "but it's your role to help them realize the truth, that they're no different than you are."

"But they are very different," he said. "I'm a Tulku, a very ancient soul. But I can't do my work if they're going to steal my energy."

His attitude didn't alarm me, especially considering his age and lack of teaching experience. It took several years before I was able to be comfortable in the same role, for it is sometimes very difficult helping people realize that they have everything within them to be happy all the time. It's easier to rely upon a guru or a spiritual master to do it for them, to give them complete power over our lives, but in my opinion, those days are over. People are discovering the power within them, and in doing so realize that they have to accept the truth for themselves. I could understand Tensin's confusion about this, and I decided that his overzealous attitude was simply the result of his inexperience, and that was something I could perhaps help him with. Maybe that was one of the reasons the Dalai Lama sent him to the desert. Perhaps I had as much to teach him as he had to teach me.

"It's difficult to have people pull on you in that way," I said to him. "And it's sometimes hard to shield yourself from all the projections people throw at you. But you'll learn, I know you will. It may take . . . "

"No, you don't understand," he said. "There are darker forces that come to play, and they sometimes use these people to derail such a high teaching. The Dalai Lama deals with this all the time. I have seen him strike out at those forces, sometimes even when they are attached to a particular person. This is the Tibetan way.

That's why the mala beads are so long. It makes for a good weapon in such cases."

He started to laugh at his joke, but it made me uncomfortable, nonetheless. I knew that there were certain wrathful deities that are honored, or even feared in his tradition, but I was worried that he was reading too much into the given situation. Once again, the fact that Lama Tensin was only fifteen years old accounted for a great deal. On one hand I could feel his profound clarity, even while talking on the phone, but there was something else that I couldn't quite put my finger on, something that I knew I would watch in the future. It didn't seem sinister, but definitely confused.

"Are Joanne and Nancy taking care of you?" I asked, trying to change the subject. "You couldn't have two more powerful women on your side."

"Yes, they have both been very helpful. And sometimes His Holiness speaks to me through Nancy. She is even aware of it when it happens. If he is happy with what I am doing then he tells me through her, and if he is angry, well, he lets me know that too."

"How does that work?" I asked.

"Oh, it's very simple. His Holiness's energy body has become entwined in mine from the years we have spent together over the centuries. When he chooses to, he can look through my eyes, or through the eyes of someone who is close to me. And if he wants to, he can speak to me through them, but only if they are a clear channel, which Nancy is. He likes her very much, I can tell."

He sounded like a fifteen-year-old boy again, not the wise master that sometimes erupted from beneath his skin. I had no real way of judging what he was saying because I had never had any experience with this, and I wasn't about to underestimate the Dalai Lama. It all made sense to me, and so I decided to believe everything I heard, at least for a while.

"Lama Tensin, I have a question I want to ask you."

"Yes, ask me anything you want."

"I don't know how much the others have told you, but I have had some amazing experiences lately with powerful psychic children who claim to have a very important message to give to the world. I think you are one of these children, and so I want to know if there is a question you want to ask. I know that sounds strange, and maybe I haven't said it right, but I believe you know what I am saying."

"I don't know what you mean," he said.

"Let me try to be more clear. The children I have met all had a question that they were asking the world, a very critical question for our time, and it was always the same. Do you know what that question is?"

There was a long pause on the other end of the phone, and I wondered what he was thinking. The other children knew what the question was without even thinking, as if it was engrained in their souls. But then again, all the children I met were from the same part of the world and were trained in the same monastery. But if it were true, and I was sure it was, then Tensin would surely express the same idea even if it was slightly different.

"I need to say something to you again," Tensin said, his voice a bit harsher than before. "I am not like the psychic children you have met. I am a Tulku. I have been here from the very beginning, and will be here until the very end of time."

"I think the same may be true of the other children I have met," I said. "In fact, I would say that the same truth applies to us all. It is not completely accurate to set one person aside as higher, holier, or even more advanced than the others. That, at least in my opinion, has been one of our biggest problems. The fact is we are the same in all the essential ways, and that is what we are asked to focus on now, not the differences."

"I agree with everything you have said," Tensin said to me. "But you will never understand what it means to be a Tulku because there are only a handful of them present on the Earth at this time. The children you have met are very important, and His Holiness has told me all about them, but I am not like them."

"So you don't know what the question is?"

"Yes, I do know what it is, but I will not say anything about it now. The time will come when it will be right for me to share it, but not now."

Something did not feel right about that conversation. My opinion about Tensin did not change, but I decided that I would pay very close attention to everything he said from that moment on. Once again Sonja's words echoed in my mind, as did the strange feeling that accompanied them. It was a warning of some kind. But why?

The tour was nearly finished and I would be returning home to Joshua Tree. At last I would meet Lama Tensin, not just speak to him on the phone. At last, I would be able to look in his eyes and see what was there, either the deep river of insight I expected, or the dark pool of confusion I feared. I was prepared for either situation, but I desperately wanted to believe as all my friends believed. By then the situation had grown beyond my expectations, for the news of the boy Lama continued to spread. Tensin was not able to leave the house without being cornered by the hoard of wandering devotees scouring the tiny town hoping to find their young guru. Joshua Tree is usually a mecca for rock climbers and alternatives, but this newest twist added a dimension no one ever experienced before. I stopped at the local cafe to buy a latte on the way back to the house and overheard a table of women comparing notes. They had searched the town for two days hoping to locate Tensin, but their search had led nowhere. Luckily, those who knew where we lived had enough sense to keep it a secret, but it wouldn't last long. Sooner or later, word would get out, and then our sanctuary would end.

I drove up the long driveway and parked the car in the usual place. As I climbed the steps that led to the front door, I could feel a strange sensation in my stomach. It was tight and hot, and I wondered if it could be explained away by something I ate, or if there was more that I didn't want to acknowledge. I looked at the cup off coffee I held in my hand, but I knew it had not caused the sensation. It wasn't anything I ate or drank that formed this knot, but something I had yet to discern.

But then I remembered how much I had missed the friends I lived with, those who held the space so brilliantly in the midst of this latest hurricane. I hadn't seen them in a month and a half, and that was enough to move me forward and in through the door. My dog Harley Krishna was the first to greet me. Then I saw Joanne coming down the hall, and Stephanie coming out of the office.

"Jimmy, you're home at last," Joanne said as she threw her arms around me. Stephanie joined us and, for the first time, I knew I had arrived.

"A lot has happened here since I left," I said, trying to understate the whole thing.

"You're not kidding," Stephanie laughed. "It's like we're under siege. We're always afraid people are going to find out where Lama Tensin is hiding, then we'll all have to move."

I could see from the look on Joanne's face that Tensin had just entered the room. I turned around and saw him for the first time. He looked exactly as I thought he would. He was nearly the same size as me and wore the traditional robes of a Tibetan Buddhist monk. His head was shaved, and his smile was as bright as the sun.

"Welcome home, Jimmy," he said. "And it is good to finally meet you."

Since I didn't know the protocol, I resisted my first urge to hug him. But before I knew it, he came to me and wrapped his arms around my shoulders. It felt good to finally see and feel the boy that had so electrified the area. And he was as precious as everyone said, a master soul in a fifteen-year-old body. We looked into each other's eyes and for a moment I was lost there, as if time stopped altogether. It was an amazing experience, and I realized why there were so many people searching the town for him.

"Yes, Lama Tensin, it's good to finally meet you as well. It's one thing to hear about all the commotion over the phone, and another to be here and feel it. This is more a hideout than a home."

"You have no idea how crazy it's gotten," Joanne said. "I have a carload of presents for Tensin, and we're constantly having to field requests for him. We have to say no to almost everyone or we risk hurting people."

"It's really crazy," Tensin said. "But this is what His Holiness wants. It helps me learn compassion. These people pull on me because they think I have something that they don't have. If they can steal it from me, then that will make them happy, or so they think."

I wanted to remind him what he said to me earlier, his insistence that he was different, that he was a Tulku and no one could relate to that. But at that moment I was far too happy to be home, and nothing else really mattered.

"Where are you going to put your things?" Joanne asked. "Your room has been . . . "

"You can put them in my room," Tensin said without realizing that he was referring to the bedroom I had lent to him.

"Yes, that would be fair since it's actually Jimmy's room," Stephanie said before I had the chance to respond.

"Of course, that's what I meant . . . and I'm so grateful."

"It's not a problem at all," I said. "I can sleep in the loft, and my suitcases will be fine there. It doesn't even make a difference."

Tensin smiled and I felt a mixture of deep love and suspicion for the boy. Part of me felt so honored to have him there, to have the ability to share the house, my room, and everything else with him. But there was another part of me that was busy watching him, as if at any moment his mask would fall off and we would discover something we didn't want to discover. It was a strange position, since he had given us no reason at all to be suspicious, especially not me. I had just arrived, while the others had been with him for nearly six weeks. If there was something wrong, they would have certainly sensed it by then. But still, the feeling persisted.

"And Matraya is grateful to have you back as well," Tensin said.

"Who is Matraya?" I asked.

"Lama Tensin has renamed your dog," Joanne confessed, unable to mask a moment of hesitation. "He is no longer Harley, but Matraya." She winked at me as if asking me to go along with it, as if it was a game we were playing to keep our guest happy.

"You renamed my dog?" It was the only thing I could say, as if my own mask had just been ripped off my face. For a second, I didn't feel like being so accommodating, as if there were limits to what I was willing to endure. My room was gone, the privacy of our home was in question . . . no problem. But to rename Harley . . . that was going too far. I took a deep breath. "If you all don't mind, he's still Harley to me. You can call him whatever you want, but I want . . . "

"He is an enlightened being in a dog's body," Tensin said. "This is very common. His Holiness has a dog that was a great Lama in his last life. He chose to be a dog in this life to serve in a new way. Matraya may have been my mother in a past life . . . I'm not sure, but he reminds me of the future Buddha, so to me . . . "

"Yes, I understand," I said as I took hold of my suitcase. "As long as Harley doesn't mind it doesn't bother me. I need to get my things out of the living room, so . . . "

I walked up the steps that led to the loft in order to get away. My head was suddenly pounding again, something that I hadn't felt since I was with the children at the monastery. I thought I had learned to control the episodes, to use the Gift in a way that would increase my awareness, not decrease it. But then the thought occurred to me that I hadn't been using it at all, for many weeks, especially since I first heard about Lama Tensin. There was a war going on inside me, and I was fully aware of it for the first time. I could feel the profound energy coming from the boy, and it was so easy to fall into it and believe everything. But there was something else happening, and I couldn't see it. My desire to believe what I had been told was as strong as anyone's, so why did I still wonder? I had experienced his profound teaching, and when I looked into his eyes, I felt the unfathomable depths. But the pain in my head told me I was blocking something, something that I didn't want to see, or to know.

Later that night I was alone with Tensin in the living room. The others were asleep, and I was glad to at last have the chance to be in the same room with him, look into his eyes, and see what I felt. The headache was nearly gone, and I was ready to open up to the Gift and see what it would reveal.

"It must be amazing to have lived and learned from the Dalai Lama for so long," I said. "When was the last time you saw him?"

"He has been touring the U.S. for a few weeks now, and I was able to join him in San Jose. It was so wonderful to be up front with all the other Lamas and feel that energy again. I have been away from the monastery for a long time now, and sometimes I miss the rituals and the company of the others. But many of them are very jealous of me, and that makes it difficult to stay for long."

"Why are they jealous of you?"

"Because it is very unusual for His Holiness to take such interest in a young Tulku like me. Most of them are sent to learn with the other high Lamas, but never with His Holiness. It was a great privilege, but one that I do not take lightly. It humbles me to be in his presence, even though I have been with him for so many lifetimes. I do not want the others to think I am different, but I am, and there is nothing I can do about it."

"What makes you different?" I asked him.

"It is very delicate," he said as his eyes widened. "In truth I am no different at all. That is the highest teaching, that we are all the same in Grace. But some of us have been on the ladder longer than others, and so we are closer to the sky. I made an agreement before time began to come here and accompany His Holiness and assist him in his work. I would not be able to do that if I was not a Tulku, or an advanced soul. That doesn't make me better than anyone else, only older, and sometimes we need older souls to guide us."

"That sounds so strange coming from a fifteen-year-old boy."

"But physical age has nothing to do with what we are talking about. The age of the body means nothing when you realize the eternal nature of the soul. Whether I am two or ninety-two, it would be the same. You would be able to see it in my eyes in either case. Look into my eyes and tell me what you see now."

I looked as deep as I could, and I was sure I could see Heaven there. And I didn't feel the overprotective concern that was present before, only a heart willing to believe anything he said.

"I see a great deal," I said. "I can see that you are telling me the truth."

"I am definitely telling you the truth. I have no reason to lie to you, or to anyone else. I am here only to be helpful, and that is why there are so many people coming to Joshua Tree now. We all need help, and that is the role of a Tulku, to help souls achieve enlightenment. It is something I will do for the rest of my life; then I will return and do it until every being has remembered who they are. It is the only thing that brings me joy, and that is how I am able to bear this dense existence. I fully remember what it was like before my first incarnation, and I remember all the thousands of incarnations since then. But there is one thing that stands out most of all, the love I have felt. I am happy to be here because it makes me feel that love, and so I will give everything to you and to the work you have started, Jimmy."

I was overwhelmed by the simple, direct way he related these truths. What could I do but turn over my disbelief and appreciate what was happening? The adventure started with meeting Marco, then the other children, and it would end with this amazing Tulku. It was difficult to believe that I was actually there having such a profound experience.

"There's one more thing I want to tell you," Tensin said. "You asked me about a question, if I knew what it was."

"Yes, I remember."

"I am ready to tell you the question now. It is so very simple, but it is also the summation of everything I just said to you. The question is, 'How would you act if you realized that you are an Emissary of Love right now?' In other words, what would you do if you realized the truth about your nature, the truth that cannot change the fact of your existence? And the answer is very simple. You would live that truth, because it would be the only thing that would make any sense at all. You would live as an enlightened being, because that's what you already are."

"There's one more part to the question," I said to him. "It's perhaps the most important part."

"Yes . . . in one word, 'BEGIN.' This is the moment to begin living in this way. This is one of the most important teachings of our time."

"Yes, Lama Tensin, I believe that. The children are all asking the same question, but now it is up to us to live it with them. That's what I have learned, and I'm so glad to be able to do it with you."

I was only going to be home for three days before leaving again for a concert in Mount Shasta, California. Now that I felt such a strong connection with Lama Tensin and was sure of his identity, it would be harder than I thought. I had learned so much from Marco and the other children, and I was sure to continue this experience now that Tensin had arrived on the scene. I was thrilled by the opportunity, overwhelmed by the Gift, and humbled by the chance to go deeper than I ever thought possible. What could I do but get the job done and return as fast as I could?

Tensin was scheduled to give a talk at the learning center on Saturday night, only two days after I arrived home. It was my job to get him there safely, keep him away from the crowd before the talk started, and then whisk him away as soon as it was finished. Joanne and Nancy had had enough experience with the crushing weight of the crowd trying to get near the Lama, and, as Tensin himself said, it was enough to wipe him out for a day or two afterwards. Now that I was back, there would be another person to redirect the onslaught. Tensin would finish his fire Puja, and I would have the car ready. Before anyone knew it, he would be gone and on the way back to the house that was still a mystery to most. It was a good plan, and I was about to find out if it would work or not.

During the drive to the center, I saw a side of Lama Tensin that I had not seen before. We were driving along the desert back roads where a passing car is rare, and Tensin decided he wanted to see how fast my Mustang would travel. The road we were on went straight for nearly ten miles, and even at one hundred and ten he still wanted more. He was a fifteen-year-old boy again, and I was being an irresponsible adult. My desire to make him happy was overriding my common sense, but I decided to let it pass, if only for a few more moments. I looked at his face as the Joshua trees flashed by and realized that he didn't get many opportunities to act young and free. He was so busy being the Tulku master that the young boy inside him was often ignored. There was no one else on the road but us, and I somehow knew we were safe.

Then something happened that I will never be able to explain.

"Do you want to see something amazing?" Tensin shouted.

"What is it?"

"Just say yes or no. Do you want to see something amazing?"

I smiled, wondering what he was going to do. "Sure, go ahead."

"Do you think we're going fast right now?"

"Yes, this is pretty fast," I yelled. "I wouldn't want to go much faster."

"But we can."

"What do you mean?"

"We can go faster, much faster," he said to me. "Here, let me show you."

No more than a second passed, but everything was different. We were still ten miles away from the center when he said those words, but as quick as I could blink we were pulling up to the front gate. I pulled to the side of the road and stopped the car a few feet from the entrance, shaking. Several people were standing there ready to walk in, and when they saw who it was, they walked toward us.

"You had better go inside," Tensin said. "Otherwise we may never get in."

"What just happened?" I asked, stunned. "What did you do?"

"I didn't do anything," he said. "We are simply here now. Nothing unusual at all. A moment ago we were there, and now we are here. I don't know why you're so surprised."

The people were only a few feet from the car, and others were coming as well, so I pulled forward and entered the gate.

When we were inside, I led Tensin to one of the trailers, and we went inside. Nancy was waiting for us there, and when we opened the door she sighed with relief. "Thank God you're here," she said. "The center is already filled, and there are still many people arriving. And I don't know if you noticed this or not, but there are dozens of people roaming around trying to get Tensin's attention before he goes inside. I'm amazed that you made it in here without them seeing you." Then she looked at me and noticed how shaken I was. "Jimmy, are you alright? You look white."

I looked over at Tensin and he smiled back at me. What would I say, even if I had the words? I didn't even know what happened, or if it actually did happen for that matter. But I didn't have an explanation, and at that moment, I really didn't want one.

"Yes, I'm fine," I said to her. "I'm just a little flushed from the heat. Don't worry about me."

"I think Jimmy is finally starting to believe," Tensin said with a wide childlike grin. "You could say he just took a fantastic leap in that direction."

"Well, I don't know what you're talking about," Nancy said as she opened the door, "but it's time for you to begin, Tensin."

They walked out the door, and I sat there with sweat pouring off my face. Was it from the heat, or was Tensin right when he said I was finally starting to believe. But I had already experienced phenomena much more fantastic than that, especially since I met Marco. But there was something different here, and I knew it. I couldn't pinpoint what it was, but my head was pounding again, more than it had been for months. I sat down in a chair and took a few deep breaths, trying to calm the heat that was pouring from my temples.

"What are you trying to tell me?" I asked myself.

No answer came, just the persistent pounding of the drum inside my head, and the feeling that I was standing in front of one of the most important doors of my life.

After a few moments, the pain was reduced by half, and I was able to leave the trailer and enter the center for Tensin's teaching. He was planning to initiate people in the Buddhist vow of Refuge, a beautiful ceremony of turning one's life over to the Divine. The entire building was filled, and many more people were standing outside the door. I squeezed by them and stood in the back of the room. Many of the people were kneeling on the floor with their heads bowed in deep reverence. Most of the others were fully engaged in Tensin's discourse, which was a mix of childlike laughter and stories and traditional Buddhist philosophy. He wasn't saying anything that I hadn't heard before, but there was a certain sweetness in his voice that was entrancing. It was so easy to trust this boy and believe everything he said. And what of my own experience, in particular the one from the previous half hour? Was it in my mind or had it really happened? And if it did happen, what did that mean? I had more questions than answers, and standing there in the back of the room wasn't helping me.

I walked back outside and looked up at the stars. The desert sky was so beautiful with the stars forming mystic clouds of glowing light, almost enough to illumine the ground where I stood.

Maybe it was real or perhaps it was just my imagination, but it felt like the light from those stars, which were billions of miles away, was actually reaching toward the Earth and lighting it on fire. Was it possible, or were they simply too far away, their wings too short to fly this far? It somehow reminded me of Tensin, the way he lived and revealed his light. Was it an illusion, smoke and mirrors that distorted the truth, or was it our own light we were feeling? The Children of Oz said it was all about the heart opening to compassion, and when that happens, then miracles are normal and natural. Why couldn't I shake the feeling that Tensin was somehow coming from a different place than they were? I wanted to believe, just as everyone wanted to believe, and I had plenty of proof. But my head told me I wasn't seeing something clearly, and that I would never know the truth until I did.

"Open your eyes," I said out loud. "It's right in front of you, if you would only look and see it."

Two days later, I was driving from Joshua Tree to Mount Shasta to perform a concert. The cell phone rang, and when I answered it, it was Joanne.

"Something very strange is happening and I don't know what to think," she said.

"Tell me."

"Well, we received a fax this morning from the woman that was taking care of Tensin before he came to us. Tensin always said that she didn't treat him well, but she had a different story. After he had been with her for awhile, she wanted to make sure she was following protocol and was treating him properly. Who knows how to take care of a fifteen-year-old Lama, right? She contacted the ashram where the Dalai Lama lives in India and received a fax from them, which she forwarded on to us. They don't know anything about a Lama Tensin. Isn't that strange? Maybe he had a different name or something, or some other logical explanation, but I'm a little concerned here."

"Maybe it's a mistake or a misunderstanding," I said, "but either way we need to find out. After all, he's only fifteen and is a minor. We're responsible for him, and we need to take that responsibility seriously."

"So, what do you think we should do?"

"First of all, where is he right now?"

"He's spending the night at Jennifer's house in Palm Desert. He won't be back here until late tomorrow."

"Didn't you say that he showed you an identification card from a monastery in New York when he first arrived?" I asked.

"Yes, and it had his picture on it identifying him as a Lama. Maybe we should call them and clear this up."

"Absolutely. I wouldn't wait on that. I agree . . . it's probably all a misunderstanding, but we need to find out. Today."

"I'll call you back as soon as I know something," she said, then hung up.

I expected my head to start pounding again, but it didn't. In fact, there was a peaceful energy pulsing through my heart, as if everything was about to make sense. I couldn't consider the possibility that Tensin was a fake. He knew too much, had too much light around him, to have fooled so many people. I was sure that Joanne would uncover the truth, and it would all turn out to have some logical explanation.

An hour later the phone rang again.

"Are you sitting down?" Joanne asked me, and in her voice I heard a tone I had never heard before. "You're not going to believe what we found out." There was a long pause, and I knew I wasn't going to like what she found. "It was all a ruse. There is no Lama Tensin and he is not a Tulku discovered by the Dalai Lama. In fact, he has never even met the Dalai Lama. I spoke to a woman in the monastery office and she told me that he has been playing this game with many people all over the country. We weren't the first ones to call. He only took a couple of classes at the monastery and falsified the ID. Apparently the head Lama had been impressed with the diligence he showed in his studies and gave him the robes as a present. That's when he disappeared, and they have not seen him since, but that certainly wasn't the last they heard of him."

"You mean, people like us calling, asking questions?"

"Exactly. I even talked to his mother, and though she wouldn't tell me much, I was able to get one vital piece of information."

"Why do I have the feeling this is going to change everything?" I asked her.

"Because it is. Lama Tensin, our sweet fifteen-year-old boy, is not a boy at all, but a twenty-five-year-old woman. He is a she."

"But that's impossible," I said.

"Why? If you think about it, it all makes sense. Tensin was overly concerned about privacy . . . that's the reason she isn't with you now, because that was the original intention, to travel with you when you returned from England. We were expecting to see a fifteen-year-old boy, and that is what we saw. The signs were there, but we didn't see them."

"But I can't believe it was all a lie . . . he, I mean she, knew too much. She spoke and wrote in Tibetan . . . at least as far as we know she did."

"Exactly," Joanne said to me. "How would we know if it was real or not? Or maybe Tensin was a truly bright person and was able to pick up on those things very quickly, or just enough to fool us."

"I have one more question," I said. "Did you ever show her the e-mail I sent out explaining my journey to Bulgaria and the psychic children I met?"

"No. Why do you ask?"

"I really need to know this. There was something I wrote in that e-mail regarding a particular question all the children ask. It's a way of confirming if they're part of what they call the Net. They all have a question they want to ask humanity, and the question is always the same, except for a few variations."

"'How would you act if you knew you are an Emissary of Love right now?'" Joanne remembered.

"Yes," I said to her. "I wrote the question in that e-mail, and a few days ago, Tensin repeated it back to me. So I need to know if she read that e-mail, or if she simply knew it."

"I'm certain I never showed it to her, and I doubt anyone else did. We had no reason to. No one has even talked to her about your experience."

"So, Tensin was a fake down to the last detail, but she still knew the question that the Children of Oz are all asking. How is that possible?"

"How is any of it possible?" Joanne asked. "How could we have been so fooled by her? We have hundreds of people who are coming here looking for the young master, and we don't know what to tell them. Do we tell the truth? It has been a mystery from beginning to end."

"And I have the feeling that the mystery is not over yet," I said. "In fact, I think that it has only begun."

CHAPTER SIX

ANGELA'S MESSAGE

It took me nearly a week to get a grip on what had happened. For over a month, Tensin had lived in my house, slept in my room and convinced everyone that she was a fifteen-year-old boy sent to us by the Dalai Lama. To this day, I cannot believe how mistaken I was, how all of us were, and how easy it was to convince everyone of something we obviously wanted to believe, but which wasn't real. The warning signs were all there, many signs, but we were completely blinded by our willingness to believe a story that was too fantastic to be true. Part of me wanted to hide and deny my involvement. After all, I only spent three or four days with her; I had been away in England during most of her race through the hearts and minds of everyone who flocked to see something that didn't exist. I could easily claim the least blame. But I also knew it wasn't that simple. I was no different from everyone else, for I wanted it to be true with all my soul. The idea that this amazing boy had come to live and work with me was too much for my ego to withstand. I threw my chips into the center of the table, but all my cards turned out to be jokers.

I returned to Joshua Tree and tried to put the pieces back together. After all the experiences I had with the Children of Oz, I found myself doubting everything. What if I was overzealous in my willingness to believe even their claims, regardless of the proof

I thought I saw. What if they were all magic tricks, and the emergence of my own remarkable abilities had nothing to do with their influence. It was entirely possible that I was set up, that they knew of my propensity to write books about my travels and actually created everything I ultimately chose to believe.

I considered this possibility for around ten seconds before it fell apart in my mind. No matter how I looked at it, there was no way I could have been set up in such a manner. Even if Marco was just an ordinary child, there was no way they could have known I would follow my intuition as far as the mountains of Bulgaria. No one could ever orchestrate such a sequence, for in the end I realized that most of the experiences I had had nothing to do with anyone else. I had followed my own inner prodding and made my own decisions. If anyone was fooling anyone, it was me fooling me.

And that is what confused me most. It was as if I had lived two separate stories, but they were bound together by one profound thread. I met Marco and the other Children of Oz, and they were as authentic as anything. The energy that flowed from these children was enough to challenge the established rules of physics, and I saw things when I was with them that would make any scientist reconsider their allegiance to the Gospel according to Newton. Even I was able to perform feats of psychic dexterity fantastic enough to win me a job on any Las Vegas stage. There was no way to invalidate these experiences, no matter how wounded I was by my most recent encounter. Lama Tensin, on the other hand, turned out to be a master of disguise, saying all the right words and inspiring enormous confidence, but in the end there was no foundation for any of us to stand on. And yet Tensin still possessed the same transformational energy as the other children I met. He had the same "juice." The first group told the truth and the second told a lie, and yet the result was the same. People were moved to experience their own Divinity, and that, after all, was the desired goal.

My friends were reeling from the news just as profoundly as I was. They were the ones who took care of him for over a month, acting as his mother in all sorts of precarious situations. When

Joanne and Nancy finally discovered the truth, they were the ones who had to deal with things. They packed her things and took them to where she was spending the night, and then the bomb fell. The game was over, and there was no way to deny the facts. But she did deny them and did everything she could to continue the charade. Even in the light of such overwhelming evidence she maintained that she was the Tulku she claimed to be, and that no one could truly understand who she was. It took her hours to even admit that she was not a boy, but a woman, and even then it was done indirectly. "I'm a man in a woman's body." In the end she was driven to the airport and put on a flight back to New York, all the while protesting that she was telling the truth.

So, where do we go from here? That was the question that kept running through my mind. It was like landing on the square that says, "Return to GO," and you pick up your game piece and, grumbling, place it at the first position again. As for me, I decided I needed to get away again, to get out of the grueling desert and visit my daughter in Chicago. Angela would be returning to high school soon, starting her sophomore year, and it would be my last chance to see her for a couple of months. There was nothing I could really do back home. The crowds were gone and the excitement had all died down. Things were exactly as they had been before Tensin arrived.

The second day I was in Chicago I decided to take Angela to Navy Pier for the day, shop a bit in the mall, then walk along the lake. It was a beautiful day, a pleasant change from the 110-degree heat of Joshua Tree. I started to think that the temperature back home was really a metaphor for the roller coaster we had just finished. When the heat gets turned up you find out what you're really about, and I still wasn't sure what it revealed about us. Maybe it was too early to tell, as if a delayed reaction would catapult us beyond the Earth's atmosphere, where we would look back and say, "Oh, it makes so much sense now." That moment had still not arrived, at least not for me, and I wondered if it ever would. It was more likely that we would look back and barely remember Tensin, blocking him from our conscious minds and not dealing with the "whys" and the "hows," the real lessons we could have learned.

But none of that really mattered when I was with Angela. I was glad to be with my "normal" daughter, without the pretense of psychic powers or an ancient Buddhist lineage. She was at the stage of ridiculing such events, far too grounded in the day-to-day activities of being a teenager to worry about such nonsense. That was exactly the attitude I needed. It helped me downplay what had happened and get a new perspective. At that moment it was hard to see past the confusing clouds that obscured the truth. When would they pass and let me see the sky again?

"You know, I could have told you something was wrong," Angela said when I told her the story. We were walking along Lake Michigan near downtown Chicago and the waves lapped against the rocks spraying our feet with tiny drops of moisture. "I could tell there was something weird about it from the very beginning."

"What do you mean?" I asked her.

"Everyone, including you, thought that this Tensin was so special, so different from all of you, and that's what made you believe him, I mean her. She probably started off telling a little story, but when she saw how much attention she was getting from it, it got bigger and bigger. You think that she was the one who made up the story, but in reality it was you."

"We didn't make up the story," I said to her. "We were just repeating what she said to us."

"I know that's what you think happened, but it really isn't. You saw exactly what you wanted to see and heard exactly what you wanted to hear. If you hadn't, then you would have noticed the warning signs and seen through her story right away. You drew her to yourself, and she played the role you wanted her to play."

She was starting to make sense. "Keep going," I said.

"What else is there to say? Of course she shouldn't have made the story up, but you were a willing participant, not a victim. And maybe you set it up to learn a particular lesson."

"What do you think the lesson was?" I asked.

"Maybe that the story you hear has nothing to do with the reality behind the story." She paused. "I can't even believe I'm saying these things . . . I'm starting to sound like you. Anyway, you're always saying that we're already enlightened, but we don't believe it. What would happen if we pretended to be enlightened? If we are already there, then pretending to be it would make it real. Does that make sense?"

"More than you know," I said. "Keep going."

"Well, Tensin was pretending to be an enlightened Buddhist monk, and it sounds like she really believed it was true. You said that everyone who hung around her felt some strong energy, just like the children you met in Bulgaria. The problem is that they were real and she was a fake. So why was the same energy there?"

"That's what I've been trying to figure out."

"I think I have figured it out," Angela continued. "She was pretending to be something that was true. Maybe the story wasn't true, all the nonsense about being a Buddhist monk and stuff, but the story behind the story was. She was so convinced that she was everything she said, that it became her experience, and then it became yours."

"How was that?" I asked.

"Because you believed it. You could only feel it if you believed it. Otherwise you would have looked right past the story and either said, 'Yeah, whatever,' or you would have not believed it at all. The other children you met believed it too, but they had something that Tensin didn't have . . . they could also feel the truth. That's why the miracles happened around them. They could feel the truth and that opened their hearts. It's like you said . . . the miracles only happened because their hearts were open, or something like that. Tensin believed it, but she didn't feel it."

"So Tensin was pretending to be something that she wasn't . . . enlightened," I said, "and that made her act and teach like an enlightened being. But the other children did more. They weren't just pretending . . . they had allowed their hearts to open so wide that they didn't need to pretend, and that was why there were so many miracles."

"That's what I think. Either that or you were all just gullible."

"Gullible?"

"Yeah . . . I bet she wouldn't have fooled me. Don't you think I would have realized that he was really a she?"

"I don't know, Angela, she fooled a lot of people."

"That's because you wanted to be fooled," she said. "But luckily you were able to feel the truth in spite of that."

"Because there was a place in Tensin that really was that truth, even though she was just pretending."

"Yeah . . . you're always telling people to pretend they're enlightened. Maybe that's how you become it, by pretending you already are."

"That's brilliant, Angela. Are you sure you're not one of these 'Children of Oz' kids?"

"No way. I'm not a freak like them. You know me, I'm totally normal."

"Okay, then let me ask you something," I said to her. "If you could ask all the people in the world one question, what would it be?"

"What kind of a question is that?" she asked.

"Just humor me for a moment. If you had the chance to ask humanity one question that would relate to what you just said, what would you ask?"

Part of her didn't want to play my game, but I sensed another side of her that did. She thought for a moment and seemed to be taking me seriously . . . a nice surprise.

"Okay," she finally said. "Here's what I would ask: 'How would you act if these things were true . . . if all this Emissary of Love stuff is real? What if it wasn't just make-believe, but really worked? Start now.'" She stopped and looked at me strangely. "That didn't even make sense," she said.

"Oh yes it did. It made a lot more sense than you know."

As I sat down to write the final part of this book I was awed by everything I learned from Marco, the children in Bulgaria, Tensin, and maybe, especially, Angela. I thought that I had everything I needed to write this story after I returned from Bulgaria, but then Lama Tensin came into my life with his bag of tricks and unintended rewards. The confusion he left in his wake opened me to an even deeper appreciation of everything I had learned from the Children of Oz, but it took my daughter, a very normal teenager, to point that out. Maybe the greatest lesson I learned is that children everywhere are leading us into our role as Emissaries of Love, no matter how they appear or act. It's natural to set certain groups aside and make them seem wiser or more valuable than the rest. But in the end, the greatest lesson is that we are all the same, and maybe this is how we step into a whole new experience of ourselves. In the end we are all Emissaries of Love, and we only need to realize and believe that fact.

The greatest lesson I learned from Marco was that I already had the Gift within me, but it needed to be awakened. The lesson I learned from the children in Bulgaria was that the door only stays open when we live our lives according to the laws of compassion and peace. The lesson I learned from Tensin was that there are many ways of doing that, but the energy of love flows according to our desire to teach only love. Finally, from Angela I learned that we're all doing the best we can, and maybe that's all it takes. The Light is already there, we are already enlightened; we just need to get out of our own way to realize that. But in the end there was only one lesson to learn, and that is what binds all the others together as one. As all the Children of Oz ask us, "What would the world be like if we all realized that we are Emissaries of Love right now? How would we change? How would we behave toward one another? And if we are willing to consider this brave new world, what other time is there to begin but right now?" It is all so simple, and yet utterly profound. Everyone is saying it, we just need to listen and believe.

I am so grateful to all the children who helped me learn these lessons, and I know that there are many more out there that will help me tighten love's grip on my soul. The Children of Oz are everywhere, in our own houses, in our own backyards and neighborhoods, even when we look in the mirror. The question is whether we're willing to listen to the question that can change our lives, not only listen but bravely respond to it. Is it about performing dramatic psychic tricks to impress everyone around us? Of course not. If those things happen on their own, then that's wonderful. But if they don't, focus on cultivating the wisdom that is at the very foundation of every Gift. Compassion. Love. Grace.

Peace. Without this wisdom, the powers mean nothing, but with it, the whole world transforms in front of your eyes.

I intend to travel and meet as many of these children as I can. Why? Because they inspire me and help me remember why I came here. Besides, life is meant to be lived and enjoyed, and I can't think of anything else I would like to do. I invite you to join me in this adventure, not by traveling with me to meet the psychic children of the world, but by cultivating the same mysterious spirit that helps us remember that we are all the Children of Oz. There's too much happening right now to sit back and watch. We need to be involved, ready to move at any given moment into a brave new Light. Are you ready? I believe we all are. That's what I learned from the children I have met, and I will never forget these lessons. I just want to keep answering the question they asked, every moment of my life. It's the only thing that really matters now.

Some time later I heard some fascinating news. It turns out that the Dalai Lama has identified a young woman as a great Buddhist Tulku. I didn't see a name, but it made me wonder.

ABOUT THE AUTHOR

James F. Twyman is an internationally renowned author and musician who travels the world performing "The Peace Concert" in some of the greatest areas of violence and discord. Also known as the "Peace Troubadour," he has been invited by government officials and humanitarian organizations to perform in countries like Iraq, Northern Ireland, Bosnia, Serbia, Kosovo, Israel, East Timor, and Mexico, as well as the United Nations in New York. He blends his unique style of music with his international reputation for drawing millions of people together in prayer to influence the process of peace in countries torn apart by hatred and war.

His ministry began in 1994, when he took the peace prayers from the twelve major religions of the world and arranged them to music. His goal was to demonstrate that all spiritual paths point to a single expression: Peace. In 1995, he was invited to perform the concert in Croatia and Bosnia during the height of the Balkan war. His best-selling book *Emissary of Light: A Vision of Peace* (Warner Books) recounts his amazing adventures traveling through the mountains of Bosnia learning the secrets of an ancient society of spiritual masters. The book has been translated into a dozen languages and was called "the second coming of *The Celestine Prophecy*" by *Variety* magazine.

Since 1995, James has helped sponsor several major prayer vigils that have been attended by millions around the world. The most famous was called "The Great Experiment," conducted from the United Nations Church Center in New York City on April 23, 1998. More than five million people, in at least eighty countries, participated in the vigil by attending small prayer circles in hundreds of locations around the world. A month earlier, he had been invited by Saddam Hussein to perform "The Peace Concert" in Baghdad, the same week the U.S. and Britain were preparing to bomb Iraq. A week later, James was invited by government officials in Belfast to sing the *Prayer of St. Francis* at Stormont Castle during sensitive peace negotiations there.

James Twyman is also the founder of the "Cloth of Many Colors" peace project, which weaves the prayers of hundreds of thousands of people from around the world into a single quilt nearly a mile long. This amazing quilt was presented at the United Nations in New York, the Pentagon in Washington, and was literally wrapped around the U.S. Capitol on September 20, 2000.

James Twyman's other books include *Emissary of Light* and *Portrait of the Master*. He has also recorded five CDs including *Ecclesia, Volume 1,* with Grammy-nominated producer Jim Wilson. James F. Twyman received his bachelor's degree from Loyola University in 1984, and a doctorate in ministry from Agape Seminary in 1997.

Programs with James Twyman

For more information on retreats and programs with James Twyman, visit his website at www.JamesTwyman.com. Starting in the spring of 2001, James has been offering an Internet-based study program on how you can access the same powers as the "Children of Oz," and how to accept your role as an "Emissary of Love." The program consists of a series of weekly lessons that will be delivered to you over a four-month period, as well as exciting retreat possibilities. Please visit the website for more details.

WALSCH
BOOKS

Visions of the Spirit

WALSCH BOOKS is an imprint of Hampton Roads Publishing Company, edited by Neale Donald Walsch and Nancy Fleming-Walsch. Our shared vision is to publish quality books that enhance and further the central messages of the *Conversations with God* series, in both fiction and non-fiction genres, and to provide another avenue through which the healing truths of the great wisdom traditions may be expressed in clear and concise terms.

Hampton Roads Publishing Company

. . . for the evolving human spirit

Hampton Roads Publishing Company
publishes books on a variety of subjects,
including metaphysics, health, integrative medicine,
visionary fiction, and other related topics.

For a copy of our latest catalog, call toll-free
(800) 766-8009, or send your name and address to:

Hampton Roads Publishing Company, Inc.
1125 Stoney Ridge Road
Charlottesville, VA 22902

e-mail: hrpc@hrpub.com
www.hrpub.com

The psychic children are with us now, and their message of peace is ready to be spread around the world. Do you know a child who exhibits amazing abilities and has a message he or she wants to share? James would like to follow up *Emissary of Love* with a collection of stories from these children or people's experiences with them. Please contact us at ChildrenofOz@aol.com for more information.